The Finest Square Mile

❖

Mount Jo and Heart Lake

The Finest Square Mile

Marcy
Gray
Colden
Avalanche Pass

[The land about Heart Lake] had been pronounced by experts the very finest square mile of woods in all the Forest Preserve's four million acres...For charm of situation it has very few equals. For accessibility to the great summits none. —T. Morris Longstreth, *The Adirondacks*

Mount Jo and Heart Lake

by Sandra Weber

Algonquin
Boundary
Iroquois
MOUNT JO

t

Wallface
Indian Pass

PURPLE MOUNTAIN PRESS
Fleischmanns, New York

The Finest Square Mile: Mount Jo and Heart Lake

First Edition 1998

Published by
Purple Mountain Press, Ltd.
P.O. Box E-3, Fleischmanns, New York 12430-0378
914-254-4062
914-254-4476 (fax)
Purple@catskill.net

Permission to reprint the following is gratefully acknowledged: Inventory on pages 78 and 80 from Melvil Dewey Papers, Rare Book and Manuscript Library, Columbia University. Excerpt on pages 82-83 from *Adirondac*.. Poem on pages 143-144 from *Adirondac*. Drawings on pages 124-125 from *Adirondac*. Original etchings copyright © by Ryland Loos.

Library of Congress Cataloging-in-Publication Data
Weber, Sandra, 1961-
    The finest square mile : Mount Jo and Heart Lake / by Sandra Weber. -- 1st ed.
        p.   cm.
    Includes bibliographical references and index.
    ISBN 0-935796-98-3 (pbk. : alk. paper)
    1. North Elba Region (N.Y.)--History.   2. North Elba Region (N.Y.)--Description and travel.   3. North Elba Region (N.Y.)--Biography.   4. Heart Lake Region (N.Y.)--History.   5. Heart Lake Region (N.Y.)--Description and travel.   6. Heart Lake Region (N.Y.)--Biography.   7. Adirondack Mountains (N.Y.)--Description and travel.   I. Title.
F129.N8W43   1998
974.7'5--dc21   98-22895
                                                                            CIP

Manufactured in the United States of America on acid-free paper. On the cover and the frontispiece and title pages: "Marcy to Wallface - Adirondack Peaks and Passes," original etching by Ryland Loos.

Table Of Contents

Acknowledgments

SEARCHES INTO THE PAST frequently reveal marvels of the present. My search for Josephine Schofield brought me to Mary MacKenzie, Sherry Osborn, Brian McAllister, and Bruce and Betty Wadsworth. These individuals provided not only advice and knowledge but encouragement and fellowship that is most welcome to a researcher who is frequently relegated to dusty basements, gloomy cemeteries, and hushed libraries. Thank you for bringing life to this story.

Many more people helped along the way. I wish to thank Derrick Pitts at The Franklin Institute; Terry M. Prior at Oswego County Historical Society; Karen Brooks, Neal Burdick, and Sarah LaPierre at the Adirondack Mountain Club; Jerold Pepper and Caroline Welsh at the Adirondack Museum; Reid Larson at Adirondack Center Museum; Nancy Berger at the Lake Placid Library; Lucille Dodds at the Lake Placid-North Elba Historical Society; Jacqueline Baker at the 1932 & 1980 Lake Placid Winter Olympic Museum; Jeff Stewart in Toronto; Annie Davis in Woodstock, Ontario; Dorothy Irving at Keene Valley Library; Edie Pilcher and Bill White at the Adirondack Research Library; Samuel Golden in Niagara Falls; Mary Hotaling; Bruce Cole; Ken and Nancy Foster; Paul Malo; Ed Ketchledge; James Goodwin; and Judy Lister. I appreciate the time and effort each of you made to assist this project.

Thank you to the many libraries, museums, and research facilities that assisted me. In addition to those mentioned above, I want to thank Archives of Ontario, Niagara Falls Library, Columbia University, Edison National Historic Site, Saranac Lake Library, New York State Library Genealogy Department and Special Collections, SUNY at Plattsburgh, Toronto Public Library, North York Library, The Chapman Historical Museum, Schenectady Historical Society, Troy Historical Society, Montgomery County Community College Library, Philadelphia Free Library, and Norristown Library.

A great amount of appreciation goes to Mary MacKenzie and Diane Weber for reading the first draft and providing valuable comments. Thank you to Neal Burdick for his editing work. And, thank you, Wray and Loni Rominger, publishers at Purple Mountain Press, for your continued dedication to preserving and promoting the grand history of New York State.

Lastly, I appreciate the support and understanding of my family and friends, especially Bill, Emily, and Marcy. I treasure the marvelous days we spent hiking and snowshoeing on Mount Jo, catching newts in Heart Lake, exploring the Nature Museum, and daydreaming at Eagle's Claw Rock.

Owners of the Heart Lake Property

1800s	Sylvanus Wells and J. & J. Rogers Iron Company
1878-1894	Henry Van Hoevenberg
1894-1895	William P. Clyde and Samuel B. Clarke
1895-1897	George Featherston
1897	Andrew J. Larkin
1897	Noah C. Rogers
1898-1900	Bronx Investment Company
1900-1959	The Lake Placid Club
	and its associated organizations
1959-present	The Adirondack Mountain Club, Inc.

Mount Jo and Heart Lake

This is the place. Stand still, my steed,
Let me review the scene,
And summon from the shadowy Past
The forms that once have been.

Henry W. Longfellow, *A Gleam of Sunshine*

HEART LAKE LURES ME TO ITS SHORES. It calls me—to jump in my car and drive north for seven hours. North—through New Jersey, past New York City, around the Catskills. North—along the Hudson and Lake George—until Route 73 leads me to Keene Valley, Cascade Lakes, and, at last, to the outskirts of Lake Placid village where Adirondak Loj Road crosses the plains and winds through the woods to Heart Lake.

I camp under the pines in a tent or a three-sided lean-to. I hike to the top of Mount Marcy along the Van Hoevenberg Trail. I climb Algonquin and Wright Peak and walk past the old lumber camp to Indian Pass.

At Heart Lake, I swim in the cool, clear water and gaze at the tall, craggy outline of Mount Jo. I scramble up the worn path to its summit and float with the raven across the open space to the treeless peaks.

In winter, I leave the tent and retreat to the big bunkroom at Adirondak Loj. I ski to Avalanche Pass, coast back, and then glide

**View from The Plains of Abraham. Mount Colden, Algonquin Peak,
Indian Pass, and Mount Jo (center, foreground).**
Photo by author.

on the Mr. Van trail to South Meadow. I snowshoe across frozen
Heart Lake and up icy Mount Jo.

These woods and waters, these meadows and mountains, are
special. The sky is bluer, the trees greener, the air crisper. Time seems
forgotten here. Strangers become instant friends. Simple food tastes
gourmet. Fireside chats are warm and intimate.

I often ask myself, "What draws me to this place?" but the answer
is not in "this place" that surrounds me. What draws me is in the past,
in the triumphs and tragedies that occurred on this square mile
around Heart Lake. Traces of romance and death, merriment and
bankruptcy, fame and fire linger about the tiny heart-shaped lake and
the craggy mountlet.

The story begins long ago, when city people began to visit the
Adirondack region. Hunters and trappers had already extirpated the
wolves. The wildest of the wilderness was gone, but beauty still
abounded. Artists, authors, philosophers, consumptives, and wealthy

tourists escaped the troubles of crowded, dirty, noisy civilization and entered a world of loveliness, solitude, and adventure.

In the summer of 1877, one tourist party included Miss Josephine Schofield and Mr. Henry Van Hoevenberg. The couple fell in love and climbed to the top of Mount Marcy, looked out over the vast countryside, and selected a spot to build their new home. They proclaimed the land surrounding the sparkling little lake "the finest square mile in which to get closest to Nature."

None could have guessed that before the end of their romance, dramatic changes would be set in motion by this couple—changes that would popularize Heart Lake and Lake Placid, changes that would create a network of trails into the Adirondack high peaks, changes that would break a woman's heart.

Portion of the square mile surrounding Heart Lake and Mount Jo, 1940s.
Courtesy Ken and Nancy Foster.

Clear Pond and The Bear

Among the beautiful waters of the wilderness,
this heart-shaped pond is one of the most beautiful.

Alfred Billings Street, *The Indian Pass*

FOLKLORE CREDITS HENRY VAN HOEVENBERG with discovering Clear Pond (now Heart Lake), but it had already been visited and had a path blazed to its shore before his arrival. Its outline appeared on maps as early as 1829, although it was unnamed. We can only speculate about the name and use of the pond but it definitely had been discovered early in the nineteenth century.

At that time the present Town of North Elba, including Clear Pond, was a part of the Town of Keene. On January 1, 1850, it was taken off from Keene and became the separate Town of North Elba. To avoid confusion, the term North Elba is used to refer to the area throughout this chapter.

The Native Americans who once hunted and summered in the area were almost certainly the first to discover the pond. In his *Historical Sketches of Northern New York*, Nathaniel Sylvester wrote: "North Elba has had a checkered history. Before and during the colonial period it was the summer home of the Adirondack hunting bands. In all the old maps an Indian village is located near the spot."[1] The magnificent chasm threading through the mountains in the southern section of North Elba became known as Indian Pass.

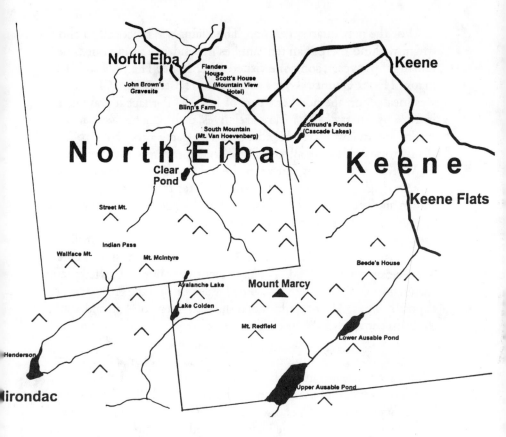

Essex County, 1876.

Beginning in 1800, a few pioneers settled on the outskirts of the present village of Lake Placid, naming their little outpost The Plains of Abraham. Archibald McIntyre[2] and his associates soon discovered iron ore in the region and, in 1810, founded the Elba Ironworks on the Chubb River at The Plains of Abraham. (The works was named for the island of Elba, a rich source of minerals from ancient times.) The little community prospered until 1817, when most of the settlers moved out because of the closing of the ironworks and the disastrous effects of that infamous "Year Without A Summer," 1816. There is no indication that settlers knew about the pond. John Richards' survey notes and map of 1812 make no mention of Clear Pond.

For the next quarter century, The Plains was practically a ghost town, with no more than ten families in residence at any one time.[3] During those years, someone visited Clear Pond. The 1829 and 1840 maps of Essex County show a small lake precisely where Clear Pond was located, on the northern part of Lot 19.[4] Perhaps it was visited in 1826 by a party of McIntyre's relatives, including his associate and future son-in-law David Henderson. The party came back to The Plains to search for an alleged silver ore deposit recently discovered by William Scott. They put up at the old abandoned ironworks.

According to Henderson's famous letter to McIntyre, a young Indian showed up at the works, produced a nugget of iron ore, and offered to guide the party to its source. Before the journey, the men spent two days combing cobbles around the Ausable River for silver. There is no mention of a pond, although their travels must have taken them close to Clear Pond. The next day the young Indian led them through Indian Pass south to Lake Henderson and the great iron ore deposits, where McIntyre founded the settlement of Adirondac and the Adirondack Iron Works. The works existed roughly from 1832 to 1858, when it was suddenly and completely abandoned.[5]

In the 1840s, a new tide of settlers came to The Plains of Abraham, which soon became named North Elba. Most have believed The Plains of Abraham became Elba and later North Elba. Town historian Mary MacKenzie has discovered that the settlement was never called Elba. It was called The Plains of Abraham until late 1849, when North Elba was chosen as the name for the post office. The "North" was necessary to avoid confusion with an Elba in Genesee County.

A few black families, including the Epps family, moved to the area when Gerritt Smith gave away lots to free blacks of the North. The offer also drew John Brown, the abolitionist, to North Elba. In early 1849, Brown and his family rented the Flanders house, just east of the present-day Adirondak Loj Road. A highway marker along Route 73 marks the location of this house. In June of 1855, the Brown family moved into the house at the present-day John Brown Historic Site.

Lyman Epps built a trail from his house to Indian Pass and guided parties on their journeys. His famous trail of open pathways and blazes crossed and recrossed the Ausable River.[6] Clear Pond would

have lain just to the side of the trail and perhaps was visited occasion-
ally.

Visitors to the area were welcomed at Osgood's Inn, the first
stopping place in North Elba. Iddo Osgood's establishment was in
business from at least 1833 to Civil War times. Osgood was employed
at Adirondack Iron Works in its early years and commuted on foot
between North Elba and Adirondac by way of Indian Pass.

Robert Scott's was the first farmhouse in North Elba to start
taking in travelers. This became a wayside inn, later enlarged into a
small hotel called the Mountain View House.

Travelers desiring to adventure through the woods needed a
woodsman guide to lead them. The "trails" were not well-marked.
At most, there were some blazes on trees, or a narrow footpath.
Guides knew the way by the streams and hills and trees.

In 1849, a party lost their way back from Indian Pass and ended
up at a pond that is not mentioned by name but by its location can
be surmised to be Clear Pond. Their story, told by the famous author
Richard Henry Dana Jr., is the earliest written account of a visit to
Clear Pond.[7] Dana's physician had advised him to go on a journey
to the mountains to cure his dyspepsia (indigestion). And so, in June
of 1849, he came to the Adirondacks with Theodore Metcalf as his
traveling companion. In Westport they secured an open wagon, two
strong mules, and a boy named Tommy to drive and care for them.
A friend introduced them to Villeroy S. Aikens, an experienced
woodsman and sportsman, who joined the group.

> June 23. At 5-1/2 A. M., before breakfast, Tommy got the mules
> ready & we were on our way Westward. The ride from Keene
> Westward is highly picturesque, thro' the ancient forests, with here
> & there a clearing & a log cabin, with small mountain torrents
> crossing the rude road, & the grand lofty mountains in sight on
> every side.
>
> About 8 o'clock we stopped at a log cabin, for breakfast. In
> this remote region almost every man who has a decent place takes
> strangers to lodge & eat, receiving compensation, rather in the way
> of a present than of regular pay. The place belonged to a man named
> Brown, originally from Berkshire Mass.—a thin, sinewy, hard
> favored, clear headed, honest minded man, who had spent all his
> days as a pioneer farmer.

This "man named Brown" was John Brown, the abolitionist, and the "log cabin" was the Flanders house along present day Route 73. After a hearty breakfast, Tommy and the wagon were sent to Osgood's tavern to wait for the trampers' return. Dana, Metcalf, and Aikens were guided through Indian Pass by a local farmer named Nash. The route lead from stream to stream, from hilltop to hilltop, through dense undergrowth and swamps, and over numerous fallen trees. Finally they found their way to the Adirondack Iron Works.

Nash returned to North Elba while the others set out for Mount Marcy. The party climbed Mount Marcy, making "the shortest passages both up & down which have ever been made." Upon return, they decided to set out for North Elba before they grew stiff and weary. The party ate lunch, had a farewell drink, and set off for the Pass with Mr. Aikens serving as their guide. He had never been through the Pass except in coming over, but being a good woodsman, he thought he was able.

They went safely through the Pass, across the first branch of the Ausable River, and then trouble started. They could not find the second branch of the Ausable. It was 6:30 and still no river. Aikens admitted he had lost his way so they struck off through the woods in the direction they supposed to be correct. They spent the cold night in an old, deserted shanty with a dinner of one small trout, which Aikens caught using a piece of his red shirt for bait.

In the morning, as they left the clearing, they found a trodden path and followed it.

> After walking an hour, we found a pond with a little skiff in it, & signs of cattle having recently been in the path. These reassured us, & after a walk of about 5 miles, to our infinite relief we came upon a high road. No dwelling was in sight, & whether to turn to the left or right we could not tell, & as houses are six or ten miles apart on these roads, the choice might be of consequence. As the left was down hill, Metcalf said "Let us go down hill, at all events,—that is the easiest," so we turned to the left, although that was contrary to the theory on wh. we had gone since we crossed the river. But instinct proved better than theory, for in a few minutes we came to a brook we remembered to have crossed on our way to Brown's, the week before, & after a two mile walk we reached his house. Three more ragged, dirty, & hungry men seldom called at a house for breakfast.

Indian Pass.
Photo by author.

The only pond in the area where the men were lost was Clear Pond. Furthermore, it was about five miles from the pond to the "high road." They probably followed a northeast course through the woods and came out on present Route 73 about two and a half miles east of Adirondak Loj Road, just about opposite the Jackrabbit trail entrance. Back then the main road was known as the Old Mountain Road and closely followed the present Jackrabbit trail behind Pitchoff Mountain and down Alstead Hill to Keene. The road through Cascade Pass was not built until 1858.

Assuming they were at Clear Pond, what about that "skiff" on the pond? Perhaps it was built and used by a local hunter or fisherman.

Could the "signs of cattle" in the path have come from the cattle or oxen of a farmer in the area? Or from deer? Or even moose? According to the famous North Elba guide Bill Nye, "In the winter of 1853 a party from Keene killed three moose up at the head of the east branch of the Ausable River....The next summer after, there was one killed in North Elba on the farm owned by L. S. Parkhurst,"[8] on the site of the present Olympic ski jumps.

Regardless of the speculations, Dana's account is the first to suggest that not only had Clear Pond been found, it was also being visited regularly.

The earliest account that mentions Clear Pond by name was written by author, poet, and New York State law librarian Alfred Billings Street. He also named the little mountain beside the pond, now Mount Jo, "the Bear." His visit probably occurred in 1865, a dozen years before Henry Van Hoevenberg's visit.

Street's account begins one summer morning as he leaves for a tramp.

> I started with a guide for Clear Pond, deep in the woods, and distinguished by many as the loveliest water of the forest. It lies toward Indian Pass, but aside of the trail to it.
>
> From a pasture south of Scott's we struck into the woods, and after crossing a brook (Meadow Brook) by an old log bridge, entered a lumber-road through the forest, with here and there a cleared space. Gradually ascending, a few miles brought us to a dead clearing, the Lower Alger Job, containing a dozen acres. A short distance farther we struck another and much smaller clearing, the

Upper Alger Job, with a decayed loghut, called Nash's Shanty, on its southern side, and on the left of the road. At the end of the Job, and near a second brook which we crossed, the road ceased, and we struck a trail through the woods. At length we came to a third and broader stream—the south branch of the West Ausable River. We passed over on a prostrate trunk, and the trail here ceasing, we skirted, by a line of blazed trees, the east slope of a wild mountain, and descending, saw through the openings of the woods the glitterings of Clear Pond.

Among the beautiful waters of the wilderness, this heart-shaped pond is one of the most beautiful. Sparkling like a gem in its depth of woods, it rejoices in its loveliness, only for the most part in behalf of the fauns and dryads. Solitude reigns generally supreme, broken alone by the fish-hawk, as he dips his dappled wing for his prey, or the deer, as it steals to the brink to taste the molten silver. We had determined to pass the night at the pond, and the guide began cutting shanty-wood for the camp-fire, upon a small point which thrust its tongue out as if to lap the diamond waters. Sunset found us prepared for the night. And what a picture the sunset painted! Whereas two mountains depicted in Lake Colden, no less than four found here their photographed features. To the west, Mount McIntyre was reflected; at the south frowned Mount Colden; in the east, old Tahawus painted its black form; while a wooded mass (the same we had skirted)—tall, save in the dwarfing presence of these eagle mountains, and called by me, in default of a better name, "The Bear,"—threw its sable counterfeit at the north. How beautiful, grand, and impressive! This little silver mirror of the woods, scarce a half mile broad by the same distance in length, holding in its heart four frowning monsters,—three of them the sublimest of the wilderness, of which one was among the stateliest in the nation. How like the human heart enshrining grand objects in its small receptacle, and showing thus its lofty capabilities, as did Napoleon,—

> "The ebbs and flows of whose single soul
> Were tides to the rest of mankind."[9]

As twilight surrounded the camp, Street reflected on the name he had given the small mountain beside the pond and wrote a poem, "The Bear." After writing the ninety-six lines, Street watched the night scene and then wearily threw himself "upon a mossy mound as in a downy cradle, and slept." The next morning they left for Scott's "once more through the pleasant woods."

Indian Pass from Ames' (Scott's), North Elba, about 1880.
Photo by S. R. Stoddard.
Courtesy of The Chapman Historical Museum.

Clear Lake from Mount Jo (The Bear), 1888. Photo by S. R. Stoddard.
Courtesy of The Adirondack Museum.

Gradually, more visitors came to the area. According to an unknown author, Scott's wayside inn became "the most prominent resort to tourists in this section of North Elba, where comfortable accommodations may be had, and intelligent directions obtained in regard to the surrounding region. It lies almost beneath the shadow of the Adirondacks."[10]

Author Charles Dudley Warner came to the area and left his mark. Supposedly, he camped at Clear Pond and failed to extinguish his campfire. The fire created the only clearing in the entire area, the spot between the present Adirondack Mountain Club lodge and dock.[11]

Another famous man, Verplanck Colvin, state surveyor and superintendent of the great Adirondack Survey, camped at Clear Pond on Sept. 7, 1873. He arrived in true Colvin fashion, pushing his men from the summit of "Cariboo Pass" by Lake Colden down through the dark, unmarked woods. "By a rapid march through the unknown forest we reached the main branch of West Ausable river before night," he wrote in his official report. "Then striking a trapping line (marked trees), the course we followed in 1869 when marching from Avalanche Lake, we concluded to make a push for Clear Pond even if it took a night march; for now on a trail, with aid of our lanterns, we could proceed with little difficulty. Accordingly, we set out and made a hard march, the trail being obscure and much fallen timber in the way. Reached Clear Pond about 10 p.m."[12]

The next day Colvin made the first measurement of Clear Pond, determining its altitude to be 2,159 feet. "The work completed, we again shouldered knapsacks and commenced our march for the settlements of North Elba, which we reached at dark that night."[13] It is not known if Colvin followed a trail or lumber road to Scott's or simply bushwhacked out to the main road.

Five weeks later, on October 14, 1873, the great Adirondack photographer and guidebook author Seneca Ray Stoddard visited the area, starting from Lake Henderson and walking through Indian Pass. After the party reached Lookout Point and started toward North Elba, the way was difficult to find. They were "often misled by seeming paths until the absence of scars on the trees warned us to retrace our steps and gather up the missing thread. On and on, until it seemed that the eighteen or twenty miles we had expected to travel before seeing a familiar landmark had lengthened out into twice that number; then in the gathering twilight we emerged from the woods in sight of North Elba, forded the Ausable—grown to be quite a river since we had left it away back toward the head—and up to Blinn's, with a sound as though a whole colony of bull-frogs were having a concert in each boot."[14]

One might think Stoddard regretted the trip. On the contrary, he wrote: "Does it pay to go through Indian Pass? I answer a thousand times yes. It costs a little extra exertion, but the experiences and emotions of the day come back in a flood of happy recollections, and the soul is lifted a little higher and made better by a visit to that grand old mountain ruin."[15]

Stoddard commemorated the day by turning back south from Nelson Blinn's farm and sketching the scene. The fine, graceful line in front of Mount McIntyre is the earliest known image of Mount Jo (The Bear).

By the middle of the 1870s, trampers, writers, and surveyors had explored Clear Pond and The Bear. A few blazed lines, paths, and trails traversed the forests in the area, but nothing foreshadowed the developments that would soon occur on Street's "mossy mound."

Mount Colden, McIntyre, Indian Pass, and Mount Jo (center, foreground)
from Blinn's, 1873. Sketch by S. R. Stoddard.

The Early Years of
Henry Van Hoevenberg

In 1869...Invention was not a recognized profession...Usually they [inventors] were regarded as eccentric, long-haired, unwashed, on the verge of lunacy and not to be trusted with money.

Roger Burlingame, *Inventors Behind the Inventor*

A YOUNG ELECTRICIAN AND INVENTOR named Henry Van Hoevenberg came to Clear Pond in 1877. This 5-foot-4-inch man had more impact than any visitor before or after him. Within three years, he purchased the property, built a huge lodge there, renamed the mountlet, and changed forever that mossy mound beside Clear Pond.

Henry Van Hoevenberg was born on March 22, 1849, in Oswego, New York, and grew up in Troy, New York.[1] Although no birth certificate has been found, the date of his birth is inscribed on the family burial monument. The Van Hoevenberg family history says Henry was of old Dutch Huguenot stock and that the family name means "from the high hills or mountain."[2] It seems Henry was destined for the Adirondacks.

His great-great-grandfather was Reverend Eggo Tonkens Van Hoevenberg, a minister in the Dutch Reformed Church. Eggo's son Henry served in various offices to aid the Revolution and then moved

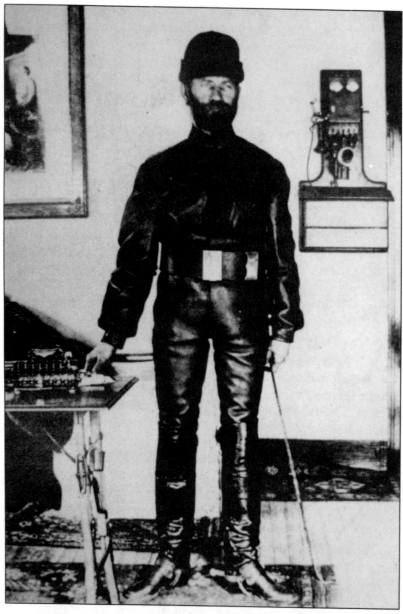

Henry Van Hoevenberg with some of his inventions, circa 1880.
Courtesy of New York State Library.

Facing page: Five generations of the Van Hoevenbergh family.

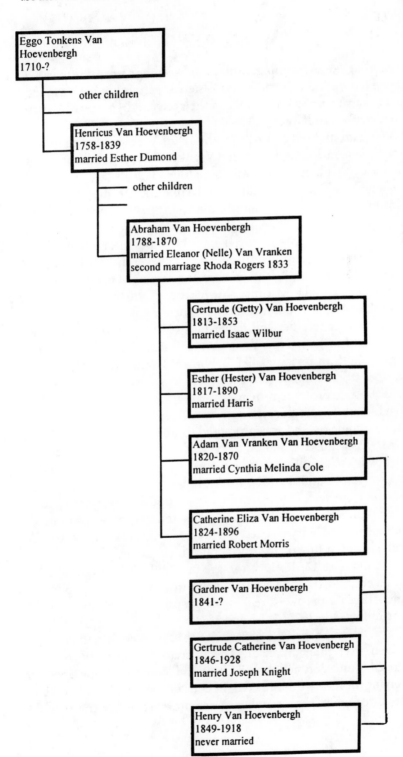

Eggo Tonkens Van Hoevenbergh
1710-?

— other children

Henricus Van Hoevenbergh
1758-1839
married Esther Dumond

— other children

Abraham Van Hoevenbergh
1788-1870
married Eleanor (Nelle) Van Vranken
second marriage Rhoda Rogers 1833

Gertrude (Getty) Van Hoevenbergh
1813-1853
married Isaac Wilbur

Esther (Hester) Van Hoevenbergh
1817-1890
married Harris

Adam Van Vranken Van Hoevenbergh
1820-1870
married Cynthia Melinda Cole

Catherine Eliza Van Hoevenbergh
1824-1896
married Robert Morris

Gardner Van Hoevenbergh
1841-?

Gertrude Catherine Van Hoevenbergh
1846-1928
married Joseph Knight

Henry Van Hoevenbergh
1849-1918
never married

about sailing sloops, farming, fishing, and keeping a store. He married Esther Dumond, a descendent of Elsie Rutgers Schuyler Vas, and bought a farm near Saratoga. One of their ten children was Abraham (our Henry's grandfather).[3]

Abraham married Eleanor "Nelle" Van Vranken and they had four children, including Adam Van Vranken. Evidence indicates that Adam Van Vranken Van Hoevenberg (our Henry's father), moved to Oswego to work at the building of the first lake steamer, *Vandalia*. Adam married Cynthia Melinda Cole and they had three children: Gardner, Gertrude, and Henry. When Henry was just a few months old, the Van Hoevenbergs moved east to Cohoes, near Albany.[4]

By 1860, the family had moved to the Seventh Ward in Troy, where Henry's father, Adam, worked as a machinist and Henry, age 10, attended school.[5] At times, his mother, Cynthia, worked as a dressmaker and his brother, Gardner, worked as a clerk.[6]

Henry's grandfather and father both died in 1870. His mother and brother moved to New York City. His sister, Gertrude, married Joseph Knight, an associate of H. B. Nims & Company, a major book and paper store in Troy. And then there was Henry.

Like other prominent men of the era, Henry began his professional life as a telegraph messenger boy. At his job in Hoosick Falls, he learned quickly and was promoted to operator. Then he moved to Lee, Massachusetts, and on to New York City. He continued to find jobs as a telegrapher since he reportedly was able to send at a rate of 35 words per minute. He apparently had no formal education in telegraphy but said, "I have spent a good deal of my spare time in studying the science, and have had access to instruments, and made experiments."[7] Henry started working on improvements to the telegraph and in July of 1871 he applied for a patent.

On October 17, 1871, at the age of 22, Henry was granted his first patent, No. 120,133 Improvement in Printing Telegraphs. He earned three more patents relating to the printing telegraph in 1872. More followed in 1873, 1874, and 1876.

The telegraph was the first device that allowed instant communication over long distances. The operator sending the message encoded it into dots and dashes (short and long clicks); the operator receiving the message deciphered the code into alphabetic letters. This system required a great number of operators trained to translate the

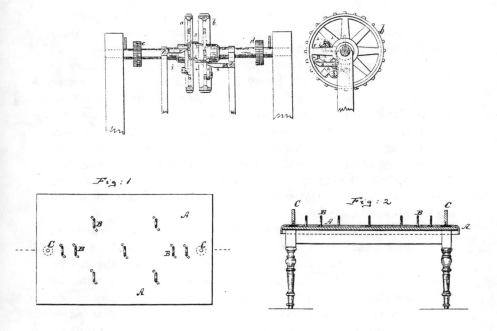

Van Hoevenberg Patents: #120,133 Improvement in Printing Telegraph, 1871; #197,504 Improvement in Parlor Croquet Apparatus, 1877.

Morse code of dots and dashes. The printing telegraph eliminated the need for operators to learn the code; the machine translated the clicks into letters and printed the result.

The printing telegraph promised to be an important instrument until the invention of the telephone made it obsolete. However, it was still useful in stock ticker and news ticker devices. Henry has been recognized for his work in this area: "The stock ticker has enjoyed the devotion of many brilliant inventors—G. M. Phelps, H. Van Hoevenbergh, A. A. Knudson, G. B. Scott, S. D. Field, John Burry—and remains in extensive use as an appliance for which no substitute or competitor has been found."[8]

In the mid-1870s, Henry worked for the Gold and Stock Telegraph Company. On September, 15, 1876, he went to work for the

Atlantic and Pacific Telegraph Company as an electrician. Shortly
thereafter, he testified in a major court case between Atlantic and
Pacific Telegraph Company (holder of Edison patents) and George
Prescott and others over quadraplex telegraphy. Van Hoevenberg
gave 145 pages of testimony regarding technical details in the case.[9]

During these years, Henry moved from New York City to
Brooklyn to Elizabeth, New Jersey. Later he became chief electrician
of the Baltimore and Ohio Railroad and spent time in Great Britain
helping the British to install their government telegraph system.[10]

Henry's inventiveness extended beyond telegraph and electro-
magnetic apparatus. On November 27, 1877, he patented a Parlor-
Croquet Apparatus: "Be it known that I, Henry Van Hoevenbergh,
of Elizabeth, in the county of Union and State of New Jersey, have
invented a new and useful Improvement in Parlor-Games, of which
the following is a specification:

"This invention has for its object to provide for various kinds of
parlor games, such as croquet, a table-cloth which, when put into
place, will constitute a perfect game-table, inasmuch as the several
arches, stakes, or similar projecting devices used in such a game are
intimately connected with the cloth.

"My invention consists in riveting, stitching, or otherwise fasten-
ing the several stakes, arches, or equivalent devices intimately to a
removable table cloth or cover, which, when placed upon an ordinary
dining-room or parlor table, will at once produce a perfect game-
board, leaving the table to its customary uses when taken off, as
hereinafter described."[11]

From 1880 to 1885, Henry was granted over 60 patents, mostly
dealing with the printing telegraph. One was assigned to American
Union Telegraph Company, four were assigned to Western Union
Telegraph Company, and twenty-five were assigned to Baltimore and
Ohio Telegraph Company.

The sale of these patents, especially those relating to the printing
telegraph, earned Henry great sums of money but did not reward
him with good health. He suffered terribly from hay fever. In 1877,
after an especially busy summer, he traveled to the Adirondacks to
seek relief.

He found relief. And he found love.

The Legend of 1877

. . .the best love story in Adirondack history.

James Goodwin

I N 1878-79, Henry Van Hoevenberg, the man affectionately known as "Mr. Van," erected an enormous rustic structure at Clear Pond. For over twenty years, his Adirondack Lodge was said to be the largest log building in the world and was heralded as a comfortable woods retreat. It welcomed sportsmen and tourists along with well-known artists, authors, and professors. Much of its success and fame owed to the romantic mystique surrounding the reason Henry built this artistic log house.

What happened in 1877 to inspire Henry, a successful electrician and inventor, to build the lodge? Godfrey Dewey, one of Mr. Van's closest friends, told the popular story which Alfred Donaldson recounted in *A History of the Adirondacks*:

> The building of Adirondack Lodge traces back to romantic begin-nings. Mr. Van's first visit to the mountains was in 1877 when, with some friends, he camped on Upper Ausable Lake. In the party was a Miss Josephine Scofield, to whom he became engaged. The young lovers were naturally under the spell of the Adirondacks, and wove them ardently into their plans for the future. They decided to climb the highest mountain and from its summit select the most beautiful spot in sight as the location for a future home—a ·

home that was also to be a house of entertainment for friends and acquaintances.

They ascended Mount Marcy, and found in the outlook some embarrassment of beautiful spots. Finally, however, they agreed upon one. It was a tiny lake that looked to them like a heart-shaped sapphire deeply cushioned in the velvety green of primeval tree-tops. It lay in utter seclusion, the mountains rising sheer from its shores. One of them was immediately named Mount Jo, in honor of Miss Scofield. The spot she chose became the site of the lodge, but she did not live to see it built. She died suddenly within the year.[1]

Ever since, people have talked and written about Henry Van Hoevenberg's tragic love affair with a Brooklyn girl named Josephine Schofield.[2] It is one of the most fantastic and romantic tales from the Adirondacks, yet the particulars are unauthenticated. Various versions of the incident have been put forth, including the sensational version best told by Eleanor Early:

> You'd think that Miss Jo's father would have been glad for her to live in such a wonderful castle with a man as worshipful as "Mr. Van." But Mr. Scofield had other plans. He wanted Jo to marry a friend of his. And when she refused, he ramped and stomped like Mr. Barrett of Wimpole Street. And Jo was so heartbroken that she did an irrevocable thing. She jumped into Niagara Falls.
>
> Descendants of Mr. Van Hoevenberg deny that there is any historical basis for this sad and romantic story, but I have found it in the accounts of the times, and so it must be true. The descendants say that "the affection between the two did not mature into the hoped-for marriage, and Miss Scofield died a sudden and untimely death."[3]

No wonder we keep repeating the story; it's a great one—sweet romance and sad tragedy set in the wilderness! But who was Josephine Schofield, and what really happened to her? Authors, historians, and storytellers have been trying to find out for decades. Accounts differ. When Maitland De Sormo wrote a comprehensive biography on Van Hoevenberg in 1967, he concluded that it is "not likely that the public will ever know exactly what happened to Josephine."[4]

Perhaps that is true, but newly discovered documents shed light upon the events of 1877 and what happened to Josephine.

In a rare interview, Henry Van Hoevenberg told a news representative in 1917: "I owe everything to the Adirondacks. In 1877, I was prostrated after a very busy summer, during which I suffered severely from aggravated hay fever. Visiting the AuSable Lakes with a party of friends, I found that my hay fever had left me, and during the two weeks that I spent there I was perfectly well."[5]

To reach their camp on Ausable Lake, Henry and his party of friends followed the broad and clear trail through the forest which ended "with a scene of rarest beauty. The path leaves the forest at the summit of a bluff, at whose feet lies the Lower Au Sable Pond, with Colvin, Saddleback, and Gothic Mountains rising sheer up from the shores."[6] The party traveled up the lake in boats and then walked a short distance to Upper Ausable Pond where they settled into one of the camps.

The popular "round trip" up and over Mount Marcy started here. Henry never described the details of his trip up Marcy, but it is likely he followed the same route taken a month earlier by a *New York Times* correspondent. The trip started by rowing up the upper pond to its inlet, where a trail led to Mount Marcy. The *Times* correspondent wrote:

> This trail is said to be not more than seven miles long, and in several places is traversed by "blind trails" leading nowhere in particular, made by older guides for the purpose of misleading and perplexing the green guides from the hotels. We had already climbed a distance which, from the time and exercise expended, seemed to have far exceeded that length...
>
> I turned to the guide to ask him how many yards it might be to the top. He seemed to anticipate the question, for before I had asked it, he announced in most encouraging accents: "Only two miles and a half to the summit, and now you'll have some real climbing!" And climbing we certainly had, of a realism that eclipsed any ideal ever conceived. Over fallen trees, through tangled thickets, over miry ledges, and up ascents with an inclination like that of the side of a house, clinging to branches and tripping over slippery roots, up, up, we go, till our voices grow hollow in the increasing rarity of the air, the vegetation undergoing a gradual change until we can look over the tops of trees; a short scramble further, and we have the proud satisfaction of standing on the highest point in the State of New York.[7]

The legend says that, on the top of this same barren rock, Henry and Josephine pledged their love to each other. They looked out over the glimmering lakes and ponds, the magnificent mountains and hills, and the green valleys. After they had picked a lovely spot to build their home, Henry said that he "journeyed over the top of Mount Marcy and across country to Clear Lake (now called Heart Lake), the site where A. L. was later built."[8]

Henry and Josephine stayed two weeks and then left the Adirondacks. Henry said that he went back to New York.[9]

Where did Josephine go? Most accounts say she returned home to Brooklyn and told her father of her plans to marry Henry. It is not surprising that Mr. Schofield would have disapproved of Josephine's choice for a husband, a wacky inventor of mechanical gadgets. A minister or doctor or sheriff—these were the choices for a proper young lady, not a man tinkering with wires and switches, jumping from job to job, town to town.

All published accounts have concluded that Josephine died suddenly within a year after that romantic sojourn in the Adirondacks, although a rumor indicated that she did not die. There was even evidence to support that rumor—a young woman from Brooklyn named Josephine Schofield. She became a school teacher and remained single until her death in 1922. Might she have been Henry's love? There is no evidence she ever visited the Adirondacks and therefore it seems that this Josephine had no connection with the legend of 1877.

The published accounts must be true—the Josephine who visited the Adirondacks died. Henry's friend Godfrey Dewey, historian Maitland DeSormo, and author Seneca Ray Stoddard wrote about her death but all were silent about its cause.

Godfrey Dewey, in his posthumous 1918 tribute to Henry, said, "And after her tragic death, closely following that wonderful camping trip, Mr. Van determined to return to the Adirondacks and carry out by himself the dream they had dreamed together."[10] Dewey did not indicate that he knew the actual cause of Josephine's death.

In 1967, DeSormo wrote: "Within a year the hapless girl died under circumstances that were politely and delicately described in a curiosity-evoking fashion: 'The affection between the two did not mature into the hoped-for marriage, and Miss Scofield died a sudden and untimely death.'"[11]

As early as 1903, Seneca Ray Stoddard published a story which mentioned Josephine's death. The story said that Henry and "a lady who, before the excursion had ended, had promised to continue with him to the end," climbed Mount Marcy and chose a site to build a castle "in keeping with the wild woods surroundings." However, their plans did not work out. "Death claimed one, but the inspiration remained and gradually Adirondack Lodge took form and place, as had been planned by the two....The devotion pledged to the one who had passed on, was given to mother and sister and to the monument that grew out of a sentiment into a visible thing of beauty."[12]

Stoddard and Van Hoevenberg were business associates and friends. It appears that Henry shared the story with Stoddard, who printed a respectable account of it. Other evidence shows that Henry did grow closer to his mother and sister at that time.

Unfortunately, Henry never told the whole story to the public. However, he did write a moving poem that was published in *Stoddard's Northern Monthly* in November 1906. "In the Star-Light" had to be a tribute to Josephine (see page 39).

None of these accounts offered a clue as to why Josephine suddenly died. Others did. Author William Wessels said she died of tuberculosis.[13] And, Eleanor Early's story said that Josephine had jumped to her death over Niagara Falls. Could this possibility, incredible and preposterous as it seems, be true?

Eleanor Early said that although "descendants of Mr. Van Hoevenberg" denied it, she believed that Josephine committed suicide at Niagara Falls. Of course, her book was not based on historical evidence and contained many inaccuracies. There were, for example, no "descendants" of Henry; he never married. As Early put it, "I take the highlights and whip them up with chocolate-covered facts to make a local history, cheap at the price."[14] Perhaps the Niagara Falls story was a thick layer of chocolate fudge! Harry Wade Hicks vehemently denied the story, saying, "Extensive correspondence proves this story is fiction. The girl did not commit suicide but returned to her home in Brooklyn."[15] He had, however, said in an earlier article, "It is true that her death was sudden—within a year."[16]

There is evidence that Godfrey Dewey, Mr. Van's closest friend, was aware of the Niagara Falls story. It appears that he had publicly alluded to the rumor. He responded to a request from Alfred Donaldson for more information about the Niagara Falls story: "I said as much about Miss Scofield as I thought wise in view of the indefiniteness of information even among Mr. Van's closest friends." He repeated the tale that the lady had a stern parent who had plans for her and that on her way home she stopped over at Niagara Falls and disappeared. He continued, "There was no proof of suicide only this disappearance...I question whether I would make any more than the allusion which I gave to the incident."[17] Evidently, Dewey did not think much of the tale and wanted to say no more about it.

Significant evidence to support the Niagara Falls story comes from two obscure sources, both written by women. It seems Henry felt more comfortable talking to women. Of course, they were not ordinary women; they were wealthy, educated, refined women. Their fascinating tales depict the events of 1877.

Helen Bartlett Bridgman was a book and newspaper writer and wife of Herbert Bridgman, a business manager, explorer, scientist, and the man whom Admiral Peary cabled the famous message "Sun." Mrs. Bridgman visited the Lodge several times, was guided by Henry on hikes, and seems to have come to know him quite personally. She wrote about one visit to the Lodge during which it appears she was told about the death of Josephine. She recalled Henry speaking to her: "As one listened to the refined voice, and learned to understand the personality of a man as appreciative of the world as the woods, one could not but be filled with tender pity for a life so thrown back on itself. Yet it was not all loss, not even the unspeakable cruel death of the loved one, since he held steadily to his ideal, and how many have been able to do that?"[18]

In the next paragraphs, she is more specific about Josephine's actions:

> Out of the heavily falling rain there rose before me the noble form of Mount Jo, bearing forever the name of her whom he loved well; of her who preferred death to separation from him—torn as she was between a stern paternal will and her heart's desire.

How could the Lady Josephine, being first of all a woman, ask for a better fate than this: to be enshrined eternally in one faithful heart—to be known for all time through a changeless mountain? Though her body was whirled in the maw of Niagara to some bleak unknown, her soul must dwell about that sacred spot in a vast peace.[19]

The second account is written by Julien Gordon, the pen name of Mrs. Julie Grinnell Storrow Van Rensselaer Cruger. She was the grandniece of Washington Irving, the wealthy widow of Colonel Van Rensselaer Cruger, and the author of several successful novels and magazine articles. One article is described in the *Adirondack Bibliography* as a "romance based on the life of Henry Van Hoevenberg."

The article, titled "Underbrush," appeared in the magazine *The Smart Set* in September 1901. Mrs. Cruger described a visit to the mountains where she decided to go to a "quaint tryst of hunters" run by a man who had a "pronounced reputation for refinement." Her host, "Mr. Ingen," was a "little man" who wore "rough leather suit and leggings."

The following is a condensed version of the story.[20]

Two days after she arrived, Mrs. Cruger found herself alone with Mr. Ingen, the "autocrat of the underbrush." The other guests had gone to spend the chilly night in their rooms. The two stood on the porch overlooking the bonfire in the road below. Mrs. Cruger recalled:

> For an hour of life our souls understood each other, and I am ingenious enough to believe that he did not tell his story often; nay, I will even go so far as to say that it did not have the ring of an oft-repeated experience. It was rather wrung from him by my eager and earnest sympathy.

Ingen explained that he and his sweetheart were never engaged. He had never known her or her family; she was Canadian. Ingen had met her on a camping trip and thought her to be very talented and beautiful, even a goddess or Madonna.

One day they wandered together through the mountains and through his glass they spied a little lake in the wilderness. Ingen said:

Van Hoevenberg Trail to Marcy.
Etching by Ryland Loos.

She fancied it. We sat down on a ledge of rock and planned...this house. How we would build it near the water, all of logs, with wings and turrets just as it stands to-day, and laughingly she told me we should live here, away from all the world. It was only for fun, you see, because when I asked her hand two weeks later she told me she was engaged to another man; that she disliked him, but that he was rich and her father desired she should marry him.

...She was trained to obedience. She dared not flout him. She told me he was strong and severe, but I think he must have been very weak. It is only weak men who torture women; they like to show their power; strong ones with intelligence use it in other channels.

Thus they parted. But Ingen could not live without her.

I heard she was stopping with some relatives in Boston. I went there; she had just left them. Two days later I read of her in the papers. It made some noise at the time. On her way back to Toronto she went to the Falls. She was last seen on Goat Island. They found her hat and book.

Ingen did not know why she disappeared at Niagara Falls. He did not know if she loved him. He received no message from her or her family. But she must have mentioned him to her family because her father tried to visit Ingen.

Her father traveled to New York to see me. I was living there then. I was in business, a young fellow. I left the city not to meet him. He would not have been safe with me. *I was afraid!*

Ingen scraped together all the money he could and went back to that spot in the Adirondacks. He bought the mountain and gave it her name. Then he bought the lake, opened a road, and built the house they had planned together.

I lived here alone and was happy, after a fashion.

...Well, my family interfered. I have a married sister. She said I would go mad if I saw no one; so, to please her, I open my doors to those who care to come. It is but a few. It is too lonely for them here. What they pay me helps me keep the place...

...those who look for anything more than amusement in society will find disappointment. I chose solitude. I am content.

Ingen thought of building a marble mausoleum for his lady but feared the intruders and tourists. Still it saddened him that her beautiful, dear body was never found and she had no burial place. "The mountain is her monument," he said.

What became of the rich man she was to marry? Ingen had a chance meeting with him years later.

Oh, he is one of your millionaires; his wife is a woman of fashion.

I am something of an inventor. I went last year into the office of a New York lawyer about a patent of mine, and there...I met him.

Yes, he was introduced to me. He shook my hand. He had never, I felt certain, heard my name; at any rate, he had forgotten it. But I knew his. His name had always been branded on my soul.

He was stout and florid, an ordinary man—think of it!—and good-natured enough. It was even difficult to dislike him much.

Mr. Ingen had a reputation among the locals as "one of them fellars that ain't sharp after money" and some "think that a sign of being cracked." Likely his reputation was earned from the story that a man offered him ninety thousand dollars for the property and he refused. Ingen explained his actions.

I am not a cheat. It is not worth the half they offered, except to me. I didn't care to clinch with the fancy of a Chicago pork-packer's foolish wife, who would have wearied of her caprice the following season and sold out to some tavern keeper for a farthing. I don't care for money; I hate it. It killed my poor love. I have lived here twenty years; she was...lost on September 14, 1876. To me it seems but yesterday, and yet it is twenty years.

That is the essence of the fictional "Underbrush" account. Clearly "Mr. Ingen" was a disguise for "Mr. Van," Henry Van Hoevenberg. Many of the details about Ingen apply to Henry. He was an inventor. He was establishing himself in business in New York City in 1877. Cruger's "quaint tryst of hunters" and "autocrat of the underbrush" are synonymous with Adirondack Lodge and Henry Van Hoevenberg as they are described in later chapters.

The most astounding part of the Underbrush story regards Ingen's lady. She was Canadian, engaged to a rich man, and met her death at Niagara Falls. Was this lady "Josephine Schofield?" A wealth of evidence presented in the next chapter confirms that a Canadian woman, who was engaged to a Toronto businessman, disappeared (and likely committed suicide) at Niagara Falls; her name was Miss J. J. Schofield. It appears that although parts of the legend of 1877 have been distorted, the part about Miss Schofield jumping over Niagara Falls is true.

Most likely, the "Underbrush" story is the closest we will ever come to knowing what really happened in 1877.

In the Star-Light
by H van H

Fair is the night,
Close at my side
Sits my darling bride,
And her eyes as the stars are bright.

Dark is the night,
Close to my breast
Is my darling pressed,
For the death-angel shows his might.

Gone is the night,
But my bride new-made
In her grave is laid,
And the day has for me no light.

Henry Van Hoevenberg, "In the Star-Light,"
Stoddard's Northern Monthly (November, 1906), 16.

Miss J. J. Schofield

Trains do not connect. Can't get home to-night. Am going crazy.

Miss J. J. Schofield

I N OCTOBER, 1877, the *New York Times, Niagara Falls Gazette, Woodstock* (Ontario) *Sentinel,* and several Toronto newspapers had an interesting but tragic tale to tell. A *New York Times* article of October 22 titled "The Suicide at Niagara Falls" reported the disappearance and presumed death of Miss Schofield.

The public showed interest in these cases of "jumping over the Falls." Every year the terrible list of victims increased with a horrible certainty and the newspapers eagerly reported the tragic but usually intriguing stories. The *Niagara Falls Gazette* reported:

> None of the family was able to account for Miss Schofield's strange act. The Woodstock (Ont.) Sentinel in speaking of the matter says "it is supposed by many that Miss Schofield had walked to the edge of the island, and becoming giddy from the rapid motion of the water, fell in. This idea is strengthened by the fact that for some time she had been troubled with giddiness."
>
> A fatal flaw in this theory lies in the location of the place from which Miss Schofield launched forth to her death. For what purpose, save that of suicide, did Miss Schofield cross over to Goat Island alone, at night, and seek one of the most exposed and distant points accessible? No woman in a healthy state of mind would

choose such a lonely walk as that for pleasure, nor seek such a place
to bathe a head that ached never so hard.[1]

The young lady, said the *Times*, had grown up in Woodstock,
Ontario, and was proficient in telegraphy and also well known as a
contributor to magazines. "Some few months ago she had to give up
her position owing to illness, and has since been staying at Staten
Island, New York State, for the benefit of her health. She was on her
way home when the melancholy occurrence took place."[2]

Miss Schofield apparently jumped over Niagara Falls on October
15, 1877. (This was exactly one year, one month, and one day later
than the date given for the lady's jump over Niagara Falls in the
"Underbrush" story.) The newspapers reported her name as Jane, J.
J., and Jennie J. Schofield, and noted that she had traveled to the
Adirondacks recently. It was also reported that she was engaged to a
Mr. C. A. Kelly of Toronto.

The answer to "What happened to Josephine?" is not in the
Adirondacks, not even in this country. The answer lies in Woodstock, Ontario, Canada, where censuses, city directories, cemetery
stones, and newspaper accounts provide a remarkable portrayal of
Jane (Josephine) Schofield's life.

In 1847, the young Francis Schofield and his wife, Ann Midgely,
took their infant son, John, and left England. Francis brought his
skills as a carpenter, joiner, and millwright to the little town of
Woodstock, Ontario, Canada. He became an active member of the
Baptist Church and was a "very reserved man and possessed many
estimable qualities which won him the respect of the entire community."[3] In the next ten years, the town grew from 120 houses and 600
people to 215 houses and 1581 people. Francis and Ann contributed
to that growth. They had six sons and three daughters including Jane
(Jennie) J., born in 1853.[4] Jane J. was to attain immortality in the
Adirondacks as Henry Van Hoevenberg's "Josephine."

Jane worked as a telegraph operator for the Dominion Telegraph
Company in Woodstock. She acquired such skill that she was appointed to the position of amanuensis (short-hand writer) in the
company offices in Toronto. She also had talent as a writer. She wrote
leading stories for one of the Toronto weekly journals and was
working on a manuscript titled *The Honest Man*. As for personality,

it is reported she had a "very jolly and uncommonly brave disposi-
tion."[5]

Her parents must have been very proud of her. Evidently her
talents also caught the attention of a prominent professional man.
Charles A. Kelly, a bookkeeper and coppersmith, planned to marry
Jane in the fall of 1877.

**Francis Schofield is #84 in center of picture of "Old Boys"
of Woodstock, Ontario, Canada, 1901 (detail).**
Courtesy of Archives of Ontario, Pamphlet 1901 #80.

Unfortunately, 1877 was a terrible year for the Schofield family.
On April 13, Jane's younger brother Frank died of consumption,
which was incurable at the time. On July 5, her sister Hannah died
after struggling with the same disease for six months. Then, Jane took
ill.

About August 1, Jane left her job to take a trip to California to
benefit her health. However, she never made it to the Pacific,
stopping instead on the sea shore of Staten Island, New York. There
she accepted a position at a branch office of the Western Union
Telegraph Company. When that office closed, she was appointed
short-hand writer in an office in New York.[6]

While in New York, Jane was under medical treatment for her
premonitory symptoms of consumption. It is likely she felt very
desperate by the end of the summer and so decided to travel to the
Adirondacks to seek relief.[7] Dr. A. L. Loomis, a prominent New
York City physician, had found the Adirondacks to be beneficial to

consumptives. The climate, soil, and atmosphere possessed advantages that helped patients to improve their condition. Dr. Loomis added: "An important feature of the treatment of invalids sent to this region is camping out."[8]

In all likelihood, Jane (Jennie) J. is the Miss Schofield who joined Henry Van Hoevenberg and the party camping out at Ausable Lakes. It seems she used the name Josephine or Jo while in the Adirondacks. Presumably her middle initial J. stood for Josephine, although there is no document to certify it. It is possible she had been using the name Josephine for quite some time; perhaps it was her pen name.

At the end of two weeks, Henry returned to New York City. Jane's health had improved in the mountain air and it appears that she returned to New York City, where she was in good health for some time. The *Niagara Falls Gazette* reported, "[She] appeared to be still further improved in health, until she imprudently ventured out and caught cold, which settled in her lungs, and necessitated imperative orders from her physician to return home."[9]

Jane boarded a train in New York City on Monday, October 15. She was traveling to Toronto but decided to stop over in Niagara Falls. Somewhere along the way she sent a letter to her father telling him that she was ill and requesting him to come and meet her in Buffalo. Unfortunately, he did not receive the letter until Tuesday.[10]

On Monday evening, Jane had arrived at Buffalo and registered at the Tift House hotel as Miss J. J. Schofield. At 6:00 she boarded a train for Niagara Falls, arriving there at 7:00. She telegraphed Mr. Kelly, "Trains do not connect. Can't get home to-night. Am going crazy." She noticed the telegraph operator observing her ill appearance and strange behavior and remarked that she had "neuralgia in the head so bad that it seemed as though she would go crazy."[11]

At 7:30 she walked out to Goat Island, telling the man at the gate that she was "an artist, and wished to see the falls by moonlight."[12] The tall, young lady dressed in black was never seen again.

The next day, several items were discovered on a flat rock at the site of the old Terrapin Tower on Goat Island near the brink of the Horseshoe Falls. They found a black bombazine sacque with a railway ticket in the pocket, a pair of black kid gloves, a purse with two keys and a torn twenty-five cent script, one cuff with a gold button, a receipted bill of the Tift House in Buffalo dated October

15, and some books with the names Tom, Willie, and Charlie Schofield in them.

Terrapin Point, Niagara Falls, about 1880. Reproduced by Samuel Golden.
Courtesy of Niagara Falls Public Library.

Mr. Kelly, Jane's fiancé, went to Niagara Falls on Tuesday. He spoke with the officials and returned to Toronto on Wednesday morning, "greatly broken down."[13] Jane's father went to the Falls on Wednesday to try to determine what happened and then returned home to Woodstock, Ontario.

No evidence was discovered to explain Jane's disappearance. The next week it was rumored that a body had been recovered below the bridge, but it was a dead horse. Jane's body was never recovered. The logical conclusion is that Jane jumped into the river and went over the falls. The *Mail* (Toronto, Ontario) reported:

> The reason given for the young lady having thus deprived herself of life is that two or three members of her family died of consumption, and she was a victim to the same disease. Knowing her malady to be incurable it is supposed she no longer desired to prolong her existence in this world, and consequently caused her death in the manner described.[14]

The reason for her suicide might have been her illness. Perhaps her helplessness and bleak outlook were compounded by her relationship with Henry Van Hoevenberg. She had met a man of similar interests in telegraphy and writing and nature. She had spent two weeks tramping and talking and dreaming with him in the Adirondacks mountains. She had spent two weeks free of illness and Father and fiancé and likely dreaded returning to those confinements.

We will probably never know what was in her heart.

The Schofield family made no grave marker or memorial for Jane. The family appears to have been ashamed of her actions. Sadly, her death was not the end of the family's misfortunes. On April 9, 1878, her brother Thomas died of consumption.[15] In just one year, four Schofield children had passed away.

The parents, Francis and Ann, held to their faith and continued on for many years. Ann died in 1902, at age 80. Francis died in 1913 in the one-story brick house where Jane was born. He was 93 years old.

Jane's fiancé, Charles A. Kelly, moved on with his life. In 1882, he married Mabel Boyd and by 1885 he was proprietor of his own business, American Copper Company.[16]

Henry Van Hoevenberg, the man Jane (Josephine) met in the Adirondacks, was never able to forget her. He remained a bachelor. He spent years building a memorial to her and lived the rest of his life near Mount Jo.

Adirondack Lodge

Oh for a lodge in some vast wilderness,
Some boundless contiguity of shade,
Where rumor of oppression and deceit----
Of unsuccessful or successful war,
Might never reach me more.

Cowper, *The Time-Piece*
(on the Adirondack Lodge brochure)

LIKE WILLIAM WEST DURANT and other affluent men who built rustic Great Camps in the wilderness, Henry Van Hoevenberg was fleeing from the metropolis. He was a "Yorker" with sophisticated tastes but he did not come to the Adirondacks woods to flaunt his social status and wealth. He came to hide from the "society" that he blamed for Josephine's death.

Henry retreated to the spot that he and Josephine had chosen and faithfully carried out the plans they had made together. He built the lodge from his own design, "and not a little by his own hands, in 1878, because of a romantic heart affair the year before, most tragic in its conclusion; and here he expected to live and die—alone, without wife, child or kin."[1]

On October 24, 1859, the administrators of Daniel Blish's estate sold thousands of acres of land to Sylvanus Wells, a large landowner, a lumberman, and a State Canal Commissioner. Among those acres was a square mile of wilderness described as parcel 81, "Lot number nineteen of said township twelve, Richard's Survey, containing six hundred and forty acres."[2]

Nineteen years later, on October 28, 1878, Henry Van Hoevenberg paid $213.33 to Sylvanus Wells for "one equal undivided third part of 640 acres of land...off from the north end or part of lot 19 in township 12 Old Military Tract, Richards survey."[3] On April 5, 1880, Henry purchased "the equal undivided two-thirds part of 640 acres."[4] He paid $426.66 to J. & J. Rogers Iron Company, who must have purchased the parcel from Wells earlier.

**Road to Adirondack Lodge, about 1890.
Notice telegraph pole at right.**
Courtesy of Adirondack Mountain Club.

For a dollar an acre Henry purchased the "finest square mile" including Heart Lake and Mount Jo. ·

Henry (Mr. Van) had already drawn up designs for the lodge in the summer of 1877. Construction started soon after he purchased the first parcel of land in October 1878. Fall was the best time to build since the ground was dry, no deep snow obstructed the site, and bark clung tightly to the trees.

The building of Adirondack Lodge was an enormous task. It becomes even more amazing remembering the distance from a main road or source of supplies. Wood materials were abundant at the site, but all other building supplies (nails, bricks, tools, etc.) had to be hauled by wagon from the Ausable Forks railroad station to North Elba.

The lodge site was another five miles from the North Elba road, so Mr. Van had to build his own road. "This road built specially for the house presented great difficulties in construction, which, however, were successfully overcome."[5] Henry started with the one-mile road to the Blinn farm and then continued four more miles through the woods, laying corduroy road through the wet sections and building a bridge across the Ausable River.

The road provided a grand show. "We and the horses turned off the main road to the south. That stately row of peaks, Tahawus, MacIntyre, Wallface, Colden, and others, with the conspicuous cleft marking Indian Pass, were all directly before us. . . . But the crown of the journey, so far, came when we entered the forest; the forest as God made it—seemingly untouched by the hand of man. For miles we drove through a dense growth of birch, beech, maple, interspersed with the wonderful family of the pointed firs, spruce, hemlock, balsam, the deciduous trees in their autumn vestments. . . . At last, after miles of this, with mosses, vines, ferns and raspberry bushes in between, the Lodge was revealed."[6]

Van Hoevenberg chose a most dramatic site for his Adirondack Lodge. "It is one of the most elevated if not the highest building in New York State, standing 2,160 feet above the sea level."[7] The building was situated to face the lake "shaped precisely like the conventional heart, the lower point of which marked the extreme opposite shore; and except where the building stood, and a few necessary open rods about it, it was all forest—literally, with its curious little lake, the 'Heart of the Adirondacks,' an accessible retreat in the very center of the woods."[8]

Accessible? If an effort was made. Guests rode trains or boats most of the way and then boarded stagecoaches for the lodge. Some arrived via Elizabethtown, Keene, Cascadeville and Ames; others came through Ausable Forks, Jay, Wilmington, and Wilmington Notch. In the 1890s, New York City guests could reach Lake Placid in ten hours by fast train. They could then board a stage for the lodge or walkers could descend to the Ausable River from John Brown's, cross the river by stepping-stones, and follow a path through the woods to the lodge road.

In 1893, Baedeker's famous guidebook described the remoteness of the lodge: "a comfortable little hotel, completely hidden in the dense forest....The view from the tower extends over an ocean of forests, with not a sign of human habitation. Beyond the hotel (to the S.) all roads cease, and the only means of communication are 'trails' through the virgin forest, sometimes followed by the 'blazes' only."[9]

Many vacationers were drawn to the big hotels with their crowds and excitement, but others came to wilderness inns like Adirondack Lodge for privacy and isolation from neighbors, stagecoaches, and intrusions. Many gentlemen found the solitude and closeness to nature refreshing after spending ten months cooped up in the city. These distinguished guests paraded down the bumpy road to the lodge.

American philosopher and psychologist William James was one of these guests. Although his favorite vacation spot was Keene Valley, James visited Adirondack Lodge several times. On one occasion he wrote to Mrs. Henry Whitman:

> There are some nooks and summits in that Adirondack region where one can really "recline on one's divine composure," and, as long as one stays up there, seem for a while to enjoy one's birth-right of freedom and relief from every fever and falsity. Stretched out on such a shelf,—with thee beside me singing in the wilderness,—what babblings might go on, what judgment-day discourse!
>
> Command me to give it up and return, if you will, by telegram addressed "Adirondack Lodge, North Elba, N. Y."[10]

Besides location, the lodge was remarkable for its size and its quality and style of construction. Van Hoevenberg was one of the first to introduce *intentional* rusticity in architecture to the Adirondack region. Earlier, hunters and loggers built temporary log cabins and shanties in a primitive manner, not intentionally rustic as a conscious choice. For permanent shelters, they built more practical finished houses of square-hewn logs or frame construction with milled lumber siding. "Local folk did not romanticize crude cabins in their midst, but the hunters' shanties in the area seemed quaint to visitors. Rusticators brought notions of Noble Savages living primitively in an unspoiled wilderness Eden—a concept absolutely alien to Adirondack families."[11]

William West Durant had just introduced rustic architecture at Camp Pine Knot, his first Great Camp. Like Durant, Van Hoevenberg employed the rustic style of construction and refined it and

Above: Adirondack Lodge, 1888. Photo by S. R. Stoddard.
Courtesy of Adirondack Collection at Saranac Lake Free Library.

Facing page, top: Mount Jo from Clear Lake about 1880. Notice dense forest of spruce and fir on upper slopes of Mount Jo. Photo by S. R. Stoddard.
Courtesy of The Chapman Historical Museum.

Facing page, bottom: Seven-story tower of Adirondack Lodge.
Courtesy of Adirondack Mountain Club.

added rustic decorative details. Were the two men acquainted with each other's work? Did they borrow details from each other? Probably not. It is likely that each individually introduced architecture styles they had seen in Europe and other areas of the U. S.

Although Van Hoevenberg used the primitive mode of a log cabin, the lodge was not "primitive"; rather, it was exotic. Its elaborate features demanded great craftsmanship; it was not hastily or casually thrown together. Guidebook author E. R. Wallace said "its construction displays marvelous skill in back-woods architecture."[12]

Progress of the construction was reported on Thursday, April 17, 1879 in the Elizabethtown *Post*: "Mr. Van Hoevenbergh, of New

York, is building a very beautiful log Hotel at Clear Pond, in the town of North Elba. The logs are carefully selected of uniform size, and the house promises to be the most perfect log structure in the State."[13]

It is said that Durant "would have his men search for days for timber with just the grain of texture which polished, would best adorn some feature of a house."[14] It seems Van Hoevenberg insisted on the same perfection, but chose the trees himself; he wore out several pairs of corduroy pants searching through the woods for just the right spruce to cut into logs for his lodge. It is estimated that more than 600 fine, straight spruce trees were felled to build the lodge.[15]

The lodge walls displayed marvelous skill in design and construction. They were entirely composed of spruce logs, left round and with the bark on. The logs in the low courses were two feet and more in diameter. The corners had projecting log ends and were saddle-notched—the upper log notched to "saddle" the one beneath. This technique usually left a sizable space between the logs, but Mr. Van required the logs laid so that they touched each other throughout their entire length and so that no marks of the ax could be seen.

Stoddard wrote, "Everything about the house or grounds evinces the cultivated taste of the owner, for the same sentiment that protected hoary tree and graceful shrub alike, made cunning joints among the logs, and left their rugged bark intact so that every pilaster, balustrade or railing is still clothed in the rich brown covering that nature gave it."[16]

Besides adding charm, the lodge's rustic decorative details served structural purposes. The elaborate porch, over ten feet wide, extended ninety-seven feet along the front of the lodge and wrapped around on the southern side. Intricate wooden railings were attached to the porch. Supposedly, Mr. Van's initials were worked into one of the railings, but no photographs show the initials.

A stairway led from the porch up to the verandah, which was decorated with the same exquisite railings. The second-floor guest room at the back of the lodge also had a balcony of rustic design.

The center gable, the column capitals, the water well, the boathouse—all served functional purposes but were adorned with rustic details to add charm. The tower best exemplified Van Hoevenberg's quest for an exotic retreat. "No practical Yankee would have built a seven-story tower; it was purely a romantic folly," remarked Paul Malo.[17]

The tower had four closed stories and three open stories and was approximately seventy feet high. Mr. Van mounted a telescope in the tower to extend the view. Guests eagerly climbed the stairs to the top of the tower for the best view of the wilderness most of them would ever see.

Clear Lake from Adirondack Lodge tower. Photo by S. R. Stoddard.
Courtesy of The Chapman Historical Museum.

One female visitor seemed greatly inspired by the view from the tower. "On that primary visit I went up the Tower and looking down upon the angelic lake and endless woods, and watching the clouds lift and fall, I knew that I must return to it again and again. The magnetism of the hills is as difficult to explain as that of sex, but the one can no more be resisted than the other. Those who will may sing the song of the sea, but the mountains every time for me! The sea is wide, but the mountains touch heaven."[18]

Van Hoevenberg did not bring extensive rustic work inside. The interior walls of the lodge appear to be of frame-construction, not log. Stoddard said, "The walls are plastered, to be sure, and noise deadened, but paint and Brussels carpeting are tabooed as not in keeping with the place."[19] The fireplaces were brick, not rough stone. Windows were large single panes of plate glass in swinging sash and

Parlor of Adirondack Lodge.
Courtesy of Ken and Nancy Foster.

Castle Rustico about 1879.
Courtesy of Lake Placid-North Elba Historical Society.

Cover of Adirondack Lodge brochure.
Courtesy of Lake Placid-North Elba Historical Society.

had upper and lower curtains and insect netting. There were no window shutters, but striped canopies were assembled when necessary.

Van Hoevenberg added a few rustic accents inside. The floors were laid in woods found in the vicinity. The doors were cherry, trimmed with arbor vitae, with the bark on. The furniture was of hardwood and some had the bark left intact.[20] Snowshoes, antlers, banjos, paintings, wooden pillars, and tennis rackets decorated the parlor.

Whereas Durant built compounds of small lodges, Mr. Van built one, large, three-story main lodge, a more difficult task. It stood three stories high, about eighty-five feet across the front and sixty-three feet deep at the T, and housed the guest rooms, dining room, and parlor. In early years, Mr. Van had separate quarters in a nearby building, Camp Comfort. Later, he moved into a room in the tower and Camp Comfort was rented to guests. Servant quarters were in a frame building behind the lodge. There were also stables, a shed near the tennis court, a sugar house, theater, laundry, boathouse and seven other buildings.

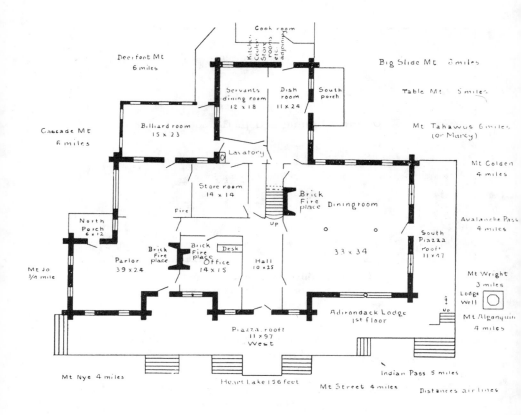

Floor plan of Adirondack Lodge

In 1881, Van Hoevenberg claimed Adirondack Lodge to be "the largest and handsomest LOG building in the United States." He also stated that it was "tastefully built, in rustic style throughout."[21]

The lodge was not the first large log building in the Adirondacks. Near Minerva, Thomas Baker's second log house, completed in 1863, was three stories high and about two-thirds the size of the Adirondack Lodge. Another log building, Castle Rustico, opened as the first hotel directly on Lake Placid in the summer of 1879.[22] It was estimated to have been eighty-seven feet long[23] and three stories high. Castle Rustico may have been as large as Adirondack Lodge but it certainly was not as tastefully built. Stoddard described Castle Rustico as "grotesque, weird and attractive."[24]

The only retreat of similar style and construction to Adirondack Lodge was Durant's rustic camp. In 1881, Stoddard called Pine Knot "the most picturesque and recherché affair of its kind in the wilderness."[25] But just two years later Stoddard discovered Adirondack Lodge and wrote, "This is a new departure in rustic architecture, and forms one of the most unique and picturesque structures in the country; a resort for nature's lovers, where nature's handiwork has been respected."[26] Between Stoddard's two reports, Wallace had said, "The Adirondack Lodge is one of the most unique designs in the line of rustic architecture that it has ever been our pleasure to inspect."[27] Paul Malo concurs: "surely it was unlike anything else in the Adirondacks, or probably anywhere else in the world, in 1879."[28]

It is unclear if Van Hoevenberg initially intended the lodge to be a business. Some evidence indicates that he built it simply as his home and as a place to entertain friends. Regardless of Van Hoevenberg's plans, tourists and sportsmen had already discovered the refreshing air, beautiful scenery, and abundant wildlife in the Lake Placid area, and paying guests started arriving at the lodge as early as 1878. Mr. Frederic H. Comstock wrote, "I recall going thro' to Adirondack Lodge in 1878 via Colden and Avalanche Lake...We reached the Adirondack Lodge quite late. It was not finished and we had to stay in the caretaker's rooms."[29]

Some part of the main lodge was open in 1880. However, Wallace's 1880 guidebook reports that the Adirondack Lodge at Clear Pond is "not yet completed."[30] The 1881 description says, "The Adirondack Lodge is now completed, has accommodations for 100 guests, and will furnish a delightful resort for tourists and invalids during the summer heats." Apparently that was wishful thinking since an ad for Adirondack Lodge said that it "will be opened for guests this summer, if possible."[31]

The public opening seems to have occurred in 1882 and was met with great excitement. A piece in the *Albany Sunday Press* exclaimed, "This new summer resort is situated on Clear Lake, a beautiful sheet of water about three-fourths a mile long, and fifty feet deep,...at the foot of Mt. Marcy...located in the midst of a dense forest of balsam, spruce, pine, and birch. This place has, this season, been opened to guests, thus supplying a want long felt by many."[32]

Boathouse at Clear Lake, August 1899.
Courtesy of Lake Placid Club Archives, Box SB-8D, Lake Placid Public Library.

Even in 1882, additions and enhancements to the lodge continued. Wallace reported, "CLEAR POND.—Adirondack Lodge. Improvements continue here, and it is destined to become a favorite
resort."[33] As Stoddard said, "[T]hese camps are *never* completed
really, for one of the fascinating features of the camp is that it is bound
by no rule of time or architecture. It expands and blossoms with the
passing seasons."[34]

By 1883, Stoddard may have visited the lodge because he wrote
a two-page description. The lodge was now in full operation with
"Capacity of house and camps, about 100. Board per day, $3; per
week, from $12 upward. Henry Van Hoevenbergh, proprietor. P. O.
address, Cascadeville, N. Y."[35]

Although the lodge welcomed anglers and hunters, it was part of
the emerging trend toward hotels in the woods providing accommodations for gentlemen and ladies and families. This reflected the
public's growing interest in nature and in the reported health benefits
of outdoor exercise. Van Hoevenberg was one of the first to provide
the rustic charm and to make "roughing it" comfortable.

Of course, the sportsmen did not welcome the tourists. One complaint in the *New York Times* said, "There was a time when only the adventurous sportsman penetrated into the wilds of the Adirondack region...[Now] it is not uncommon for a lady to make the trip through the woods."[36]

Sportsmen criticized Mr. Van for "bringing the first bathtub and tennis set to the Adirondacks and for trying to force such extravagance into the woods."[37] But the women and children liked playing as wilderness pioneers at the old-fashioned well and the shaggy boathouse. Some of the women even tramped into the woods and climbed mountains. Upon return, they relished in comforts seldom found indoors in the wilderness.

The lodge had the luxury of men's and ladies' indoor bathrooms with hot and cold running water. Large brick fireplaces warmed the large parlor, office area, and dining room on the first story. A billiard room was in the rear of the building.

The second story had a library, five fireplaces, two bathrooms, and fifteen bedrooms. The third floor had seventeen bedrooms, four with fireplaces. The room prices ranged from one dollar for a 9x9 room to three dollars for an 11x19 room with a lake view.

Each room had an electric annunciator, which guests could use to summon the office until 11 p.m. Sometime in the 1880s, telegraph

Tennis Court at Adirondack Lodge. Mr. Van on horse at far right. Photo by S. R. Stoddard.
Courtesy of Adirondack Collection at Saranac Lake Free Library.

lines were run to the lodge. Before that time, Henry went to the Mountain View House in North Elba to use the telegraph equipment. He signed the register in 1880, on the same page as Dr. E. L. Trudeau, of Saranac Lake sanitorium fame, and Verplanck Colvin. Henry signed again in 1881, 1882, 1883, and 1885.[38]

In the early days, summer guests dined in an open-air dining room. The lodge brochure read, "Good substantial mountain fare will be provided, suitable to the country—trout, venison and other game in season. No attempt at French cookery will be made; but everything will be perfectly prepared. Fresh milk, eggs, etc., in profusion..." What to wear to dinner? "As there is never any attempt at display in dress at the Lodge, guests need not bring elaborate wardrobes with them. Mountain costumes for ladies, and rough, serviceable suits, with blue flannel shirts, for gentlemen, are perfectly in order."[39]

According to one guest, "Adirondack Lodge spelt two words marvelously well, freedom and peace. You could be very drowsy in that soothing air, sleep solidly all night and fall into reveries during the day...From 10 p.m. until 8 a.m. the place was as silent as the grave, and the man could once more know the deep, dreamless rest of childhood."[40]

After a peaceful night's sleep, guests were free to lounge on the porch or to partake in any number of outdoor activities. There were lawn tennis courts and roque courts (croquet played on a hard surface) in an opening near the lake. Swings and arbors were hidden among the trees.

Guests could enjoy quiet recreation by boating on the lake. Or by sipping water—"A well at the door with old-fashioned wheel and bucket furnishes the best tonic to be found here or anywhere else."[41]

A short mile walk down the road was a branch of the Ausable River. Other fishing streams were just another mile or two. "Small speckled trout are found in abundance in all the streams," reported one guest.[42]

Being a horse person, Mr. Van offered saddle horses, buckboards, and teams on hire for his guests. A bridle path wound through South Meadow to Edmunds Ponds (Cascade Lakes), eight miles away.

Another popular amusement was climbing to the top of Mount Jo, a forty-five minute scoot. Many referred to it as the most view for the smallest effort. Stoddard declared, "The view from Lookout [on Mount Jo] toward the south is the finest mountain view in the Adirondacks."[43]

For those who wanted an excursion to the high mountains, this was the place to start. Mr. Van proclaimed, "It is the headquarters for mountain climbing in the Adirondacks."[44] Fifty miles of trails commenced from the lodge to the wild lakes, waterfalls, peaks, and passes. The most famous was a seven-mile trail to the summit of Mount Marcy. According to Wallace's 1882 book, "'Old Bill Nye,' the intrepid guide and mountain explorer, has cut a trail direct to the summit of Mt. Marcy, enabling one to make the ascent from the 'Lodge' within 5 hours. An exquisitely beautiful cascade (discovered by Nye, and christened 'Wallace's Falls,') is encountered *en route*."[45] Nye was probably trying to flatter Wallace, but the name did not stick; the waterfalls were called Crystal Falls by Mr. Van and are now Indian Falls.

Guides such as Edmund Phelps, Bert Hinds, William Young, Bill Nye, Willard Streeter, Eugene Smith, and Charles Wood were available for hire at the lodge. Mr. Van himself often guided or accompanied camping excursions. He was known for his keen instincts in the woods, humorous story-telling, and superb food. This was another of the few criticisms of Mr. Van; he dared "to maintain that real and tasty food might be managed on a camping trip instead of the usual diet of hard tack and salt pork."[46]

His guests certainly did not complain about his broiled steaks, fresh apples and oranges, or hot coffee. One time Mr. Van brought a pail for coffee on a hike up MacIntyre (Algonquin) Mountain. A woman guest raved that "Leather Stocking built a fire…and made excellent coffee in a pail suspended over the blaze by a stick. No beverage in Brooklyn, no spiced wine from storied cellars, could touch that drink, the poetry of the brown bean."[47]

Adirondack Lodge welcomed many prominent guests, such as photographer and author S. R. Stoddard, philosopher William James, and painter Samuel Colman. Author Archibald Knowles also visited:

> The following morning turned out to be rainy, and it was a most desolate scene which they saw from their windows. Dense clouds

hung over the mountains, and the pouring rain was cold, dreary
and discouraging.

They were not to be deterred, however, from pushing on, but
started in a carriage for Adirondack Lodge. It was a ten mile drive
to Clear Lake, the first portion being along the beaten coach-road.
Presently the road turned sharply to the right, and soon they were
driving through a dense forest, the single road-way soaking with
wet, and the foliage of the trees brushing them continually with
their wet leaves. Then they emerged at a little clearing, beside a
beautiful quiet lake, lying silent and black at the foot of the highest
mountains in New York State, where was the pretty Adirondack
Lodge, built entirely of logs, rough and unfinished, but beautifully
fitted and joined together.

It being impossible to walk that day, Chap and the Sport spent
the day on the piazzas, or sitting by the cheering wood-fire blazing
merrily in the office. On the porch was a group of four, playing
euchre by the hour; and it was not long before the players and the
tramps knew each other.

That night a large fire of logs was built in the road in front of
the house, the flames darting up and lighting the faces of those near
it, while the somber, black depths of the forest around remained
in the deepest shadow. Inside, the "euchre players" and the tramps
sat and "warmed up" to each other, and with the aid of some fine
cognac brandy and some malt, any distinctions existing between
Columbia, Harvard or Pennsylvania University men, or the clerk
of the hotel and the bell-boy, disappeared, and it became a thoroughly democratic and genial gathering. A right jolly crowd of
chaps they were, too, and many a witty thing was said, so that it
was much later than they had intended, when the tramps "turned
in."[48]

Van Hoevenberg had not only built a grand marvel of rustic
architecture and construction, he had also created a refined wilderness
Eden. "Every season hosts of people came there, and there they
learned to know the glory of the Adirondacks from one who understood them thoroughly in their primitive majesty. And many there
were, who, coming into these hills tired with life's grind, and weary
of the sham and hypocrisy of the over-civilized communities which
they knew, sick in body and in spirit, caught a new glimpse of what
it means to live, and went back to their work with a fresh hold on

themselves and a clearer understanding of the things that are worth while.''[49]

Herbert Eugene Hinds (guide) and Henry Van Hoevenberg, about 1900.
Courtesy of Mary MacKenzie.

Top: Henry Van Hoevenberg.
Courtesy of Mary MacKenzie.

Above: Mr. Van against white pine.
Courtesy of Adirondack Mountain Club.

Right: Mr. Van and other trampers on Mount Jo trail, about 1902.
Courtesy of Lake Placid Club Archives, Box SB-65A, Lake Placid Public Library.

The Nineteenth Century
Mr. Van

There is one thing you always remember
About a man more than any other.
Sometimes it's a trick of his hand or eyes,
Or an old coat, or a dangling muffler;
And after a while in the neighborhood
A man comes to mean just that one queer thing
That sticks in the memory...

Jeanne Robert Foster, *Ezra Brown*

H ENRY VAN HOEVENBERG, Mr. Van, is remembered as "the man in leather." People recall him dressed in one of his colored leather suits, black leather boots, and leather visor cap riding on his saddle horse.

Mr. Van explained to a newspaper man how he came to own this queer clothing:

There was a great deal of rustic work about Adirondack Lodge, aside from the immense logs of which it was built, which necessitated much search in the thick woods for appropriate trees, roots, and stumps. A new corduroy suit lasted less than a week, and another one fared no better. Seeing that my wardrobe was rapidly vanishing, I sent down to New York and had a complete suit of brown calfskin leather made, which lasted not only until the Lodge was finished, but for many years thereafter. In fact, it was still in good order, though badly scratched when the Lodge was burned in 1903. I found the material very well adapted to the weeds, but I got tired of wearing a single suit, so that I had other leather suits made of this material in varying colors. At the time of the burning of the Lodge, more than a dozen such suits of mine were destroyed. It has since become a favorite material for winter wear here, but I think I may fairly claim to be the pioneer in the fashion.[1]

No wonder Mr. Van was often referred to as a colorful fellow!

Apparently Mr. Van wore different attire for different occasions. When he went into the woods, he wore soft smoke-tanned buckskin trousers, for not only were they comfortable but they also "wore like iron." For everyday wear, he dressed in tanned calfskin trousers, which would almost stand on their own without him in them. With them he usually wore a gray flannel shirt and high Hessian-type boots. He completed the outfit with a leather jacket, leather cap, and leather bowtie.

For storytelling and other full-dress occasions, he had one or two suits of soft tanned buckskin, beautifully fringed and beaded. Sometimes he wore white buckskin with his black patent boots. One woman remarked that it was "a welcome change from the ugly male costume of the day."[2]

Mr. Van's personal appearance was described as "luxuriantly bearded and browed, stocky and muscular."[3] Author T. Morris Longstreth described his friend as short, stocky, and grizzly but also temperamental and said his keen eyes could show anger or gentleness.[4]

A female guest recalled being greeted at the lodge with gentleness "by the real host, in leather cap, coat and boots, who loves the mountains only a trifle more than his books....[He] looks as though he might enjoy a gay little dinner, or the opera, not less than the rest of us, who may not have his rarer capacity for the prolonged solitude of the woods."[5]

Van Hoevenberg shared his solitude with his horses, especially a beautiful horse named Jack. Every day he rode through South Meadow to the Cascadeville post office to get the mail for Adirondack Lodge. The North Elba post office was closer and had a road leading to it, but Henry preferred clearing a horse trail through the woods to Cascadeville. He always seemed to prefer the scenic path.

Mr. Van had one curious rule regarding animals at the lodge: "No dogs allowed in the house or anywhere upon the grounds."[6] However, in 1881 Mr. Van paid fifty cents in dog taxes for having one dog at the lodge. The next year, no dog tax was levied, so evidently the dog left.[7] What did Mr. Van have against dogs? He probably did not want dogs around the lodge because he now owned cats.

Of course Henry's pet cats were extraordinary—one could tell colors. "The cat, from Madagascar, with a Maltese coat, six claws and the appropriate name of Sextus, begged for food on her hind legs like a dog, and also recognized difference in tints. She would pick out from the primary colors the blue every time.

"There is a reason, however," confessed Mr. Van. "The packages of catnip from the drugstore are always blue. Still, I think it is a remarkable evidence of intelligence."[8]

Henry was also known for a remarkable intelligence and "His companionship and leadership on the trail were always eagerly sought. His enthusiasm, his cheerfulness, his knowledge of the woods, made him the best of guides, and his gift for weaving and telling a tale made him a boon companion."[9] One guest recalled that "The man was small, but well-proportioned, full of mettle, and how he could climb! When the rest were at the end of their tether, he only smiled serenely and bounded ahead, leaving far behind a sighing, gasping, groaning crowd."[10]

It has been said that Henry's personality was what kept guests coming back for more. But others have told of his fierce anger and refusal of guests who did not please him. His reputation scared J. L. Harrison when he visited the lodge in 1894. Finally, Harrison went up to Mr. Van's room in the tower and inquired about his Indian costumes. "That softened Mr. Van and with a broad smile he brought out costume after costume after costume, up to about 50 garments, all different, some beautiful in embroidery and bead work, given or bought, and from all parts of the U. S."[11]

Henry Van Hoevenberg enjoyed donning a costume to entertain his guests, preferably in the outdoors. Every Wednesday evening, guests gathered on the porch and Mr. Van told stories and recited verses in front of a huge campfire. This storytelling ritual had started during the construction of the lodge in 1878. Mr. Van recited "The Legend of Indian Pass" to entertain the workmen on that cold

Henry Van Hoevenberg with horse, 1896.
Courtesy of The Adirondack Museum.

Christmas night. The verse became a classic and was published in 1888 with the last page marked "Camp Comfort, December 25th, 1878."

Newspapers of the time credit Van Hoevenberg with preserving some of the old legends and stories of the Adirondacks[12] but most of Van Hoevenberg's stories were his own creations, taken from his numerous escapades in the woods and embellished by his fertile imagination. Some of his stories and poems were published in *Stoddard's Northern Monthly* magazine in 1906-8. A fabulous collection of seven stories was published as *Told Around the Campfire* in 1967 by Maitland DeSormo.

Mr. Van also wrote a complete book called *The Crystal City or The Wreck of the Western Star*. It remains unpublished, but one copy of the manuscript survives at the New York State Library. It is an amazing book to behold—typewritten and bound in a leather hardcover. Gilt lettering displays the title and the author's name.[13] The 252 pages reveal an adventure that revolves around Gilbert Mayfield's trip aboard "The Western Star," a steamer sailing to Africa. Gilbert's hunting trip is postponed when a storm wrecks the ship in the West

Indies. Gilbert and a few other passengers, including a lovely lady, find themselves marooned on a strange island with caves filled with blocks of crystals.

Besides writing and serving as host at the lodge, Van Hoevenberg continued to fuss with inventions. He patented several inventions, including a copying apparatus, two optical toys, and a few electric lamps and lamp-lighting devices.

A most interesting patent was granted on June 27, 1893, for the Billiard Chalk Cup. "In playing the game of billiards, in which smooth ivory balls are propelled across a horizontal plane surface by being forcibly struck by the convex end of a wooden rod termed a 'cue,' it is necessary at frequent intervals to apply a layer of chalk-dust to the tip of the cue, to prevent the latter from slipping upon the smooth surface of the ball when a stroke is made."[14]

When necessary, the player would rub a piece of chalk over the tip of the cue. This task could be messy and soil the player's hands. Henry's invention took care of the problem.

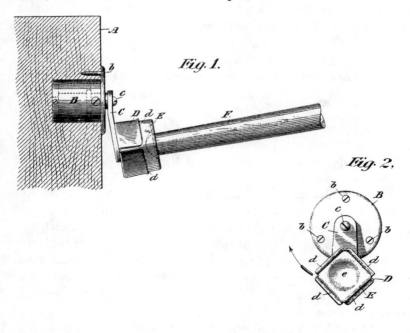

Patent #500,360 Billiard Chalk Cup, 1893.

"When it is desired to chalk the tip of a cue, the player presses the cue F against the hollow or depression e, as shown in Fig. 1, and then revolves the arm C, together with the chalk E and its holder, through one or more revolutions, as for instance in the direction indicated by the arrow in Fig. 2. The tip of the cue is by this means covered uniformly and evenly with a thin layer of chalk-dust, ground or abraded from the face of the mass of chalk E."[15]

Sometimes Henry mixed inventing with writing. In 1898 and 1899, he patented several electrical devices including electric branding devices, an electrically driven vehicle, and a trolley for electric railways. Then he wrote the poem "Trolliphobia," which pokes fun at the trolley car (see page 72). Stoddard published the poem in *Northern Monthly* magazine in June 1906, just one year after Stoddard had patented an improved electric trolley!

Unfortunately, Henry's patents put him in financial trouble. "Like most inventors he was not remarkable for commercial shrewdness, and was prone to get into lawsuits."[16] Patent infringement lawsuits were very common among the inventors and communication companies of the time; one prominent lawyer handled 600 patent infringement lawsuits. Henry lost many of his lawsuits; eventually the costly litigation depleted his finances. "The inventive, versatile, refined, temperament which may inherit or make money is not necessarily the one to conserve it—that temperament is seldom practical."[17]

As early as 1885, Henry took out a mortgage on the lodge property. He took out another in 1887 and a third in 1893.[18] All three mortgages appear to have been from friends trying to help him through hard times.

Finally he had to sell Adirondack Lodge to cover his debts. On January 13, 1894, Henry sold the lodge to William P. Clyde and Samuel B. Clarke of New York for $3,000 and subject to mortgages of $4,500. It is recorded that he sold "that piece or parcel of land with the lakes, mountains, buildings and lodges thereon. . .all the personal property. . .including all furniture, equipment, utensils, books, pictures, boats, wagons, and other chattels except only the wearing apparel, firearms, and sword."[19]

Although Mr. Van had only the clothes on his back and a few weapons, he still had a job. Mr. Clyde and Mr. Clarke arranged for

Henry to lease the lodge and continue as proprietor. Henry handled the lodge advertising with Stoddard and continued to pay taxes on the property.

Exactly what the arrangements were is not known. On paper it looks as if Van Hoevenberg sold the lodge for a few thousand dollars, a property said to have cost at least $60,000 to build.

On October 19, 1895, the property was sold to George Featherston of Jay.[20] The new owner retained Mr. Van as innkeeper, but that did not solve Henry's financial problems. On February 18, 1896, the *New York Times* "Business Troubles" column reported: "Albert J. Wise has been appointed receiver in supplementary proceedings for Henry Van Hoevenbergh of 147 West Eighty-eighth Street on the application of Charles MacLaughlin, a creditor for $4,185." The article described the sale of the lodge and said: "Mr. Van also transferred his house and furniture at 147 West Eighty-eighth Street in October last to Smith & Featherston for a debt of $1,200....He has taken out 120 patents in the United States, but has sold nearly all of them."

Mr. Van was either very desperate or very careless with his financial affairs. He seemed to be practically giving away his possessions. However, if we believe Cruger's "Underbrush" story, Mr. Van did not care about money. "I hate it. It killed my poor love," he supposedly said.

Featherston sold the lodge property to Andrew J. Larkin of Staten Island on February 15, 1897.[21] The next day, Larkin sold it to Noah C. Rogers of the city of New York.[22] Mr. Rogers kept it one summer and it then became the property of the Bronx Investment Company, owned by Mr. Rogers.

Mr. Van paid the taxes in 1896 and 1897, but the property value dropped in both years.[23] The new owners were not keeping up the buildings and Mr. Van had no money. It is unclear if Adirondack Lodge was even open for the summer of 1897. Stoddard still ran an ad for the place and listed Van Hoevenberg as the proprietor, but it was not the usual ad. By 1898 Stoddard reported: "At present writing attempts to get information as to future occupancy has failed, but the place is picturesque, even in decay, and well worth a visit to see." He says the enterprise was financially unsuccessful and that Henry was "finally obliged to abandon the effort."[24]

On June 1, 1898, W. W. Pierce signed a lease to run the lodge for three years. He may have opened it for a short time in 1898, but definitely opened it for the summer of 1899. Stoddard's guidebooks for 1899 and 1900 said: "The new proprietor aims to make the Lodge a comfortable place for parties who may wish to spend the summer months in a quiet, healthful and restful place among the mountains, and extends a cordial invitation to all tourists to take the charming drive, at least, and visit the Lodge, assuring all of a cordial welcome."[25]

When Mr. Van left his beloved lodge, he went to work at the Lake Placid Club, as explained in the next chapter. The man who had developed into a charming hotel host, skillful trail builder and guide, and masterful storyteller and writer went back to his earlier occupation as a telegraph operator. He probably cared little about losing the money or the job, but leaving the lodge and Mount Jo must have been dreadful.

Like Durant, Van Hoevenberg was forced to sell his rustic lodge due to financial misfortune. The famous Great Camper Durant was bankrupt in 1904, lived another 30 years and ended up serving those who had once worked for him. Van Hoevenberg lived another 25 years after his bankruptcy and he, too, never regained his fortunes or social prominence. But he did manage to stay close to his Mount Jo.

Trolliphobia
by H van H

I took the steamer and sailed away—
Sailed for many a seasick day;
Travelled to distant lands afar
Just to get rid of the trolley car!
    The trolley car—the trolley car—
    The ricketty, racketty trolley car.

To far Patagonia's dreary waste,
I steamed away with the greatest haste,
And said as the steamer crossed the bar,
"Now I've got rid of the trolley car."
    The trolley car—the trolley car,
    That nerve-racking, bell-ringing trolley car.

I asked the way inland as quick as I could,
As neat and polite as a stranger should.
The native replied, as he lit his cigar:
"You'd better get into that trolley car!"
    That trolley car, that trolley car,
    That South American trolley car.

In wild Sahara's sunburnt land,
What could be safer than piles of sand?
"Here my quiet no bell can mar—"
Just then whizzed past me a trolley car—
    A trolley car—a trolley car,
    A dried-up, gritty, old trolley car.

I fled to the land of the Arctic zone—
Nothing but ice in that land is known.
But on the North Pole was a big cross-bar
Supporting the wire of a trolley car!
    A trolley car—a trolley car,
    A snow-bound, frozen-up trolley car.

Henry Van Hoevenberg,
"Trolliphobia,"
Stoddard's Northern Monthly (June, 1906), 91.

Melvil Dewey.
Courtesy of Lake Placid Club Archives, Box SB-8, Lake Placid Public Library.

The Beginning of the Dewey Era

The lives of most librarians present no problems of interpretation. Most of them lead relatively placid existences...But Dewey was different.

Fremont Rider, *Melvil Dewey*

MELVIL DEWEY is world-renowned for his creation of the Dewey Decimal Classification System once used in many libraries. He also made contributions in education, spelling reform, and metric reform in this country. In the Adirondack region, he is well known as the founder and spirit of the Lake Placid Club. Many people also remember his role in the Lake Placid Club's discrimination policies. These parts of Dewey's life have been documented in several biographies, the most recent being *Irrepressible Reformer: A Biography of Melvil Dewey.*[1]

The little-known story is Melvil Dewey's close association with Heart Lake. Actually, he named it! He also owned the original Adirondack Lodge and, later, built a new lodge. The Lake Placid Club and its associated companies held title to the Heart Lake property for fifty-nine years. The personal passions and peculiar rules of Melvil Dewey found their way from the Lake Placid Club to Heart Lake and some still linger there today.

Melville Louis Kossuth Dewey was born December 10, 1851, the youngest child of Joel Dewey and Eliza Green. He grew up in Adams

Center, Jefferson County, New York splitting wood and tending cows with his siblings Marion, Marietta, Manford, and Marissa.

Besides doing chores, the young boy kept busy studying and helping at his father's store. The activities listed in his diary include "practicing telegrafy."[2] At age fifteen Melville decided what he wanted to do with his life; he would devote himself to education. At age seventeen he became a teacher at Toad Hollow school, near Adams Center.

Melville soon developed a passion for efficiency and identified his life's ambition—reform. His three causes became The American Library Association, the American Metric Bureau, and the Spelling Reform Association. He even simplified the spelling of his name by dropping the final "le." Later, he shortened his last name to Dui, but then changed it back.

He graduated from Amherst College in 1874 and earned a master's degree in 1877. After starting a few "businesses" of his own, he accepted a position as chief librarian of Columbia College in 1883 and later founded the first library school there. In 1889 he moved to Albany and served as secretary of the Regents of the University of the State of New York and New York State librarian. Every place he went, Dewey made great advances to his causes, but his ego usually allowed him to push too far, too fast. He believed his honorable, altruistic motives excused his mismanagement of business funds, circumvention of institution rules, misrepresentation of facts, and lack of tact. Thus, most who knew Dewey were either devoted supporters or dogged enemies.

Besides their political problems, the Deweys had problems with their health. Melvil suffered from hay fever and his wife had rose-cold. They sought relief in the Adirondacks and started a resort there in 1895. As T. Morris Longstreth put it, "The Lake Placid Club was sired by a sneeze."[3]

Dewey recalls, "We wanted to devote our lives to the cause of education and one way of doing this was to help the educators. If we could give them an opportunity to find health, strength and inspiration at moderate cost, we knew we would be helping them."[4] The Lake Placid Club was intended to secure seven things: "health, comfort and convenience, quiet and rest, congenial companionship, attractive recreations, beautiful natural surroundings, and as moderate living expenses as is consistent with high standards in each of the above chief aims."[5]

From the beginning there was good-natured ridicule of "that darned literary fellow" and his unbelievable rules. No drinking. No sale of cigars. No gambling. No elaborate jewelry or fashion. No noise after 10 p.m.[6] How could he possibly succeed?

But succeed he did. By 1911, the club had a house count as high as 1,000 in summer. He owned 6,000 acres and had 200 buildings, 22 farms, a post office, a library, a printing press, greenhouses, sports facilities, and numerous other operations.[7] Dewey claimed the club succeeded not despite those rules but because of them. The character and atmosphere of the club—its simplicity in dress, architecture, and furnishings; endorsement of sports and amusements; emphasis on health and safety; and careful selection and treatment of employees—endeared it to members.

Lake Placid Club, about 1909.
Courtesy of New York State Library.

Although Lake Placid Club was intended for professors, teachers, writers, preachers, and librarians, its standards "quickly attracted families of culture and refinement whose ample means made moderate cost a secondary consideration, and whose demands for more and better facilities led naturally to a spiral of higher costs."[8]

If members demanded more, Melvil Dewey would not stand still. He often said, "When a tree ceases to grow, it begins to rot."[9] So he decided to meet the new needs by adding "branches" to the original Club.

Sometime in the 1890s, Dewey and Van Hoevenberg must have met. We can only imagine the conversation that ensued between these two extraordinary men. Dewey must have liked Van Hoevenberg because he gave him a room and a job as telegraph operator and postmaster at the Lake Placid Club.

When Mr. Van left Adirondack Lodge and moved into the club, he met Melvil's only child, Godfrey. The ten-year-old boy immediately took a liking to the peculiar woodsman and the two became life-long friends.

Perhaps at some point Mr. Van suggested the idea of buying his beloved lodge for a branch clubhouse. The club needed a forest branch and Melvil Dewey must have been impressed with Mr. Van's ingenuity, wit, spunk, and woodsmanship. How could the plan fail with Mr. Van appointed resident manager and club forester?

As usual, Melvil took immediate action. He created the first branch, the Forest Branch, by buying Adirondack Lodge on September 12, 1900.[10] Clear Lake was renamed Heart Lake to avoid confusion with Lake Clear Junction north of Saranac Lake. The legend goes that it was named Heart Lake by Mr. Van and Josephine in 1877. Perhaps Mr. Van did refer to it that way, but he always wrote Clear Lake. The Lake Placid Club was the first to print the name Heart Lake.[11]

The 1901 Club Handbook encouraged members to visit Adirondack Lodge at Heart Lake: "The builder of the Lodge [Mr. Van] with a force of men spent the winter in needed restorations and renovations and it will open July 1, 1901....New equipment, boats, livery, furniture, linen and china supplement the renovation of the building."[12]

An inventory for Adirondack Lodge, dated September 15, 1902, indicates the lodge cuisine and atmosphere. Among the items were:6 lemonade pitchers, 2 waffle irons, 2 omelet pans, 2 dozen bread pans, 1 ice cream freezer, 1 coffee pot (gray granite, 2 gallon), 2 gravy boats, 34 salt shakers (only 32 pepper shakers), 12 syrup jugs, 4 dozen scalloped drop cake pans, 1 set of tubes (1 each for Eclair, Macaroons, Lady Fingers, Wafer, and Crinkle & Jumble), 2 pudding steamers,

Mr. Van at the Club, 1903.
Courtesy of Mary MacKenzie.

134 dinner plates, 170 knives, 310 forks, and spoons (257 tea, 116 soup, 130 table, 16 coffee).[13]

The lodge remained open from July 1 to November 1 in 1901 and 1902 with Mr. Van residing as host. According to Godfrey Dewey, the lodge "flourished as in the palmiest days of its earlier history, and the spirit of the woods radiated from its doors as of old....And the old Lodge trails wore smooth again with the tramp of happy feet."[14]

On the surface, the Adirondack Lodge may have seemed like the lodge of old, but it was different. With club ownership came club standards. Only club members and those introduced by them could rent rooms for a week. Others were welcome to temporary stays if they could provide "satisfactory references."

The remoteness of the lodge was slipping away, too. Farmers had cleared land farther and farther into the forests. The first three miles of the lodge road now ran through open fields. Communication with the outside world was fast and convenient via long-distance telephones installed at the lodge. Daily carriages brought guests and mail from the club to the lodge. There was no longer any need for Mr. Van to ride his horse to Cascadeville.

Mr. Van was having problems with the changes. He was not accustomed to working for someone else and business at the lodge was not up to expectations. In a letter to Mr. Van dated January 12, 1903, Melvil Dewey complained about "continually pouring money into a losing place." He told Mr. Van, "You know all the facts and the danger of selling or shutting up the Lodge if we can not make a better showing than we have so far....I am inclined to lay more stress on your advice than on any one's else because you know the circumstances better and I believe are thoroughly loyal to the beautiful place."[15]

Mr. Van's efforts to "make a better showing" proved futile. On June 3, 1903, Adirondack Lodge burned. Melvil Dewey's grand Forest Branch was destroyed.

The Fire of 1903

This was the worst holocaust of its kind in the history of the state.

Harry W. Hicks

THE ADIRONDACK FOREST was highly flammable in the spring of 1903. There was very little moisture on the ground from melting snow because of light snowfall throughout the winter. Help did not come from spring rains; less than a quarter inch of rain fell between the middle of April and the end of May. Fires began breaking out and fire fighters fought to extinguish them, but many remained, smoldering in the dry duff. Fortunately, there was not much wind to stir up the cinders and spread the fires, but the lack of wind also meant that the smoke hung in the air. "Cinders fell in Albany, 150 miles away from the chief fire center of Lake Placid. It has been reported that smoke from the Adirondacks caused concern in Washington, D.C. Darkness like that of an eclipse of the sun fell on northern New York, and consternation and panic seized upon populations of many villages and isolated communities in the mountains."[1]

This was a time of few telephones, poor roads, no automobiles or fire trucks, and few fire towers or fire roads. Most telephone and telegraph lines were down. Men ran from town to town fighting back the fires with no word of how their families and farms were surviving. The women at home were frightened by the constant smoke in the air and worried about the men off battling the blazes. In some places it was necessary to sleep on the floor to escape the heavy smoke hanging in the air.

"The weather is warm and sultry, and this, together with the dense smoke and intense heat of the flames, makes the work of fighting the flames unusually difficult and disagreeable," the *New York Times* reported.[2] Some men worked "fifteen hours a day for a number of consecutive days, some to be prostrated later by sickness following the long strain and complete physical exhaustion. The various communities and the State owe such men a debt which pay checks can not cancel."[3]

Despite the frequent fire outbreaks, hikers still came to climb Mount Marcy.

> The time came in May 1903 when three other kindred souls (Emmons, Hubbel and Dickinson) joined me in planning a trip to Adirondak Loj and a climb to the top of the state. How to get there was a problem, as in those days before automobiles a trip of twenty miles or so seemed quite an undertaking. So it meant either hiring a team, hiking or riding bicycles. The first was too costly for us, the second seemed too slow and so bicycles were the answer. Later we regretted this decision as the roads were rough and sandy and we eventually had to walk most of the way anyhow and drag the bikes besides.
>
> The last stretch as we neared Heart Lake was through beautiful, untouched, virgin timber. When within a short distance of the Loj (the original one, located between the present Loj and the parking area), we were brought up short as we met a strange looking little man dressed all in black leather—even to his bow tie. He introduced himself as Henry Van Hoevenberg and, hearing that we were there to climb Marcy, took us in charge and escorted us to the Loj....
>
> The next day we started up the Marcy trail. The climb to the top was a strenuous one as we were soon floundering in ten or twelve inches of snow and, near the top, we encountered deep snow drifts.
>
> Our views from the top were very limited as that was the year of the big fires and we were facing heavy smoke clouds in every direction. But—we were standing on top of the state and our dream had come true!
>
> Sliding and slipping and very wet, we arrived back at the Loj in the late afternoon and, before the light failed, were taken up the

Loj tower and were introduced to Mr. Van's famous reflecting telescope—powerful enough to clearly see the nails in the survey-ors' rustic tripod about five miles away! In the evening, after another delightful dinner, we again mounted the tower and had a good scope look at the moon…

The very next week the Loj and that entire area were destroyed by fire. As I look back I am thankful that we had the good luck to make the trip when we did.[4]

Good luck, indeed! Destiny, perhaps. The writer, William G. Distin, who spent one of the last days at the old Adirondack Lodge, would be the man to design a new lodge in 1927.

In some parts of the Adirondacks, railroad locomotives sparked the dry forest into flames. Near Lake Placid, the fires were likely started by the practices of farmers, loggers, and sportsmen. Farmers cleared land by burning debris, a practice known as fallowing. Although this practice was forbidden in April and May, many farmers burned fallow in the spring of 1903. Lumbermen sometimes left piles of treetops and dead wood, which provided favorable conditions for the spread of fire. Fishermen built smudge fires to keep away the black flies and mosquitoes and left them not fully extin-guished. Another possible cause for the fires was the carelessness of many woodsmen in their habit of pipe smoking. Some fires were deliberately set by persons angry with private preserve owners or state ownership of timber lands, by firefighters who could earn good money fighting fires, by hunters to grow grass to attract deer, by berry pickers to improve the berry harvest, and by persons who enjoyed watching the excitement of the fires and fire fighting.

In the Lake Placid area, firefighting started about April 27 and continued through May and into June. "About May 28 to June 3 (the latter being the worst day) high winds occurred in the Adirondacks, fanning smoldering fires into activity. As a result fire fighting became generally ineffective. The woods became so hot and smoky that everyone was compelled to take refuge in the clearings and to confine his efforts to an attempt to save the threatened cottages, camps, hotels, and farm buildings. The destruction of the entire region seemed not at all improbable, for in the dense pall of smoke it was impossible to tell where the fires were."[5]

On June 3, Mrs. Williams, the wife of the lodge caretaker, went into Lake Placid to visit the dentist. Mr. Van had been out camping the night before. He had searched for signs of danger out near McIntyre, but found none. Unfortunately, the danger was about to find him.

Three separate fires raged toward Adirondack Lodge. The first came from the north. "In April a farmer near Lake Placid lost control of a fallow fire. It caught in the duff and smouldered there until the 3d of June, when an unusually strong wind fanned it into a surface fire, which traveled 8 miles in two hours and a half. It leaped clearings and streams. At times it proceeded through meadows, making a path only a few feet wide, and then, driven by the wind, burst into a roaring conflagration, which in a few hours devastated a tract 6 miles long by 3 in width."[6]

A second fire had been burning since May 15 when it "had gotten away from workmen who had been burning out stumps on the Lake Placid Club Tablelands Farm."[7] This fire swept over and around Mount Jo. Ironically, this fire started at a Lake Placid Club property and would be largely responsible for burning another Lake Placid Club property.

A third fire swept from Keene through Cascade Pass and "was probably set, as sometimes happened in those days, by unscrupulous men seeking employment as fire fighters."[8] The fire burned over Cascade Mountain and scorched large sections of Porter Mountain, then continued west.

As the fires headed toward the lodge, a call for help came from South Meadow. "Mr. Van sent two men and a team with axes and shovels to help at South Meadows but, before they reached the bridge [over Marcy Brook], they were cut off by the fire from the north and had to turn around and lash the horses up the hill to get back to the Lodge."[9] The fire consumed several lumber camps at South Meadow[10] and raged up into Klondike Pass. "In this last remote region a cache of dynamite had been stored for lumbering purposes. Proof of the southeast boundary of this particular fire is that this dynamite was exploded on June 3, the culminating day of the battle."[11]

Back at the lodge, Mr. Van mounted his seventy-foot tower and tried to look out over the smoky tree-tops. He could just see the flames surging down from Mount Jo. He saw that he was being hemmed in by the fires and that the lodge was doomed.

Mr. Van jumped to action. He called to his men to help him carry down his large telescope, placed it in a boat, and pushed the boat out into the lake. He took his lathe off its bench and placed it in another boat with an armful of leather clothing. Then he threw the table silver into shallow water. Next he brought out the model of his "Kemigraph" that he was working on and placed it on a rock in the clearing. Finally, he emptied the stable of six horses and locked the doors.[12]

At last the men from South Meadow returned and all thoughts turned to escape. They started on the trail to Indian Pass with Mr. Van in the rear of the retreat. Before long, Mr. Van told Frank Williams, the caretaker, "I've got to go back," and away he went.[13] Williams waited and then went back and found Mr. Van prepared to go down with the lodge. "It was a foolish bit of bravado, if you like, and directly traceable, no doubt, to overstrung nerves, but showing a touching depth of affection for a place—and a place he no longer owned but merely loved."[14]

Mr. Van drew a revolver and told Williams to leave, but the loyal friend refused to leave without him. This brought Mr. Van back to reality and the two men gathered a few belongings and ran for their lives. They barely escaped the flames.

"Meantime the fire from the northwest had come around Mt. Jo and crossed the tote road so they had to run thru it. It was a measure of emotional tension they were under that a live coal as big as a bean fell on the back of Mr. Van's hand and burned its way in flush with the skin before he noticed it."[15] They ran hurriedly around the north side of Heart Lake and on to the entrance to the Indian Pass trail. A brief sense of safety was provided by a stand of mature hardwood, which would burn much more slowly than pines.

The two men managed to run two miles to safety at Hennessy's lumber camp near Rocky Falls. They roused the men there, and all went about a mile farther up the tote road toward Indian Pass and waited. Luckily, the fire did not follow the men to Indian Pass. The wind changed direction as the fires converged on the lodge. The fire turned off toward McIntyre and then east toward Marcy.

After hours of waiting in the darkness, the men heard a great crash and knew that the lodge tower had fallen. "The Adirondack

Lodge had passed into the Land of Things that Were," wrote Donaldson.[16]

The men walked back to the lodge the next morning. The ground was black and almost every tree was burned. All that remained of the lodge were some large cellar holes. Fifteen of the buildings had been destroyed. The only building still standing was the flimsy bark shelter containing a half box of dynamite! When Mr. Van returned to the site, he stuffed the dynamite under his coat and ran across the smoldering ground to the lake. He tossed the explosives into the water.[17]

Mr. Van in the rubble of the Adirondack Lodge after the fire of 1903.
Courtesy of *Lake Placid News*.

"The level of the cold lake had been lowered about a foot; and in the shallow margins along the east shore, dead fishes had been boiled to rags."[18] The deep well had gone dry.

The horses had taken refuge in the sugar bush and were totally unharmed. The sugar maples were the only hardwood trees standing within a mile, although a six-foot ribbon of fire ran through the grove and burned the sugar shack.

Mr. Van's six-inch reflecting telescope was retrieved from the boat and mounted on the roof of one of the buildings at the Lake Placid Club. Later it was replaced by an eight-inch telescope.

Mr. Van refused to leave the ruins. For days he wandered around the wilderness. Godfrey Dewey came home from school to comfort him. Together they saved as many of the big pine trees as they could from the smoldering fire.

Mount Jo was burned bare to the rocks from base to summit. "Near the Mt. Jo shore of the lake, three giant white pines, more than four hundred years old, had survived, apparently because their tops were above the crown fire and their roots were in earth so wet that the ground fire did not run there."[19] But even those three trees were soon lost. The next year a club crew was dispatched to Heart Lake to clean up and salvage lumber, and without warning cut them down.[20]

A *New York Times* front page headline reported "Flames Raging in Tinder-Dry Forests: In Adirondacks Vast Stretches of Woods Are Destroyed." The article declared that "The forest fires in the Adirondacks, for a time believed to be under control, have burst forth with renewed fury, and vast stretches of the dried timberlands on the mountains of New York are being swept bare by flames."[21] An article on page 2 reported: "The forest fires last night destroyed Adirondack Lodge, a Summer hotel, about two miles from Lake Placid, on the North Elba Road."

Some relief came on Friday, June 5, when the winds subsided. But the fire that burned the lodge was not completely extinguished until rain came on Sunday, June 7. The rain was almost continuous and seemed to put out the fires and render the wood so wet that more fires seemed extremely improbable. The *New York Times* reported: "Considerable rain fell in the Adirondacks this forenoon and this evening....As rain had not fallen in fifty days, to any appreciable extent, when it did come there was tremendous rejoicing."[22]

The six weeks of fire fighting was finally over. "Hundreds of men dropped their tools that day and slept the sleep of utter physical exhaustion. Another week of strain would have beaten down all defense."[23]

Relief was felt around the state. In Glens Falls a shower finally broke the drought. "The smoke in the atmosphere cleared away almost entirely and for the first time in several days blue sky was to be seen."[24]

Within a week after the rains extinguished the fires, the state Forestry Department reported via a *New York Times* article that the burned areas were much less extensive than previously reported and the loss of valuable virgin timber had been exaggerated.[25] Of course, the article also explains the department's motivation: "The Forestry Department is interested in the maintenance of Summer business in the Adirondacks, and insists that nothing has occurred that should in the least deter any one from going to the mountains as in previous years.

"Col. Fox [State Superintendent of Forests] says the Summer visitor will see no changes in the woods as he looks out upon them from the hotels, cottages, and camps. The only indication there will be to the visitors of the fires that have occurred will be seen along the line of the railroads."

Another headline about Lake Placid read, "Not One Black Tract To Be Seen." The article reported that "the Adirondack forests remain practically unchanged so far as their charm for summer visitors is concerned. In but one instance did the flames approach near enough to any of the big summer resorts to do any damage, when Adirondack Lodge was burned. Even in that case the reports of the affair were grossly exaggerated since a resident of this place said to have met his death fighting the flames there actually lost his life through accidentally falling down a flight of stairs."[26]

The other hotels and their surrounding forests were untouched and as beautiful as ever, claimed the article. "[A]nd the lovers of the woods now returning by each train find no change in the pretty walks, drives and shore nooks where they have passed so many pleasant hours in past seasons." It concluded: "The fires in the Adirondacks, while extensive, have been confined principally to State lands and the large unsettled tracts. While the loss on timber has been well-nigh beyond estimate, the loss on other property has been nominal."[27]

Was this ignorance of immense forest damage or an attempt to salvage summer tourism? These articles certainly were not describing the Heart Lake area. A rare personal account documents that there definitely was "change to the pretty walks." A month after the fire, two hardy souls took an excursion via the entrance to the lodge. Howard Goodwin and Joe Twichell planned to take a wagon into the lodge area and then climb Marcy and over to Elk Lake.

> We arranged for a guide, a man by the name of Burt Hines [Bert Hinds], to take us through the burned forest. Driving to the ruins of the lodge, we started off through the blackened woods. We had never seen anything like it. For mile after mile, there was nothing but charred blackness. Every bit of the Marcy trail was burned away, as was the forest floor covering of leaves, duff and everything else. It was a cool, cloudy day, and those woods certainly looked dark. Hines was a good guide and led us to the edge of the burned forest right where the unburned Van Hoevenberg trail came down to what is now called Phelps Brook.[28]

Obviously the Heart Lake area suffered great damage. And much destruction occurred to hiking trails. Blazed trees acting as trail markers were gone; bridges were gone; tree tops and charred logs covered the trail; "widow-makers" threatened to fall on courageous trampers. "The popular Van Hoevenberg Trail to Marcy was destroyed throughout its lower half. So chaotic were the remains of Bill Nye's great work that no immediate effort was made to restore it."[29] It was not recut until 1919.

The trail up Algonquin was destroyed and the trail on Mount Jo was lost. Trails to Dix, Cascade, and Porter were also gone. In the years following the fire, hikers managed to find their way to the peaks by following the many lumber roads built to salvage burned timber and to reach the unburned areas.

The *New York Times* immediately reported that "Adirondack Lodge will be rebuilt at once. In the instance of Adirondack Lodge it will take two or three months to replace the building."[30] Melvil Dewey notified Lake Placid Club members that as soon as possible new trees would be planted and a new lodge would be built to make the blackened spot lovely once again.[31]

According to Stoddard, it did not take long for Mr. Van to return to his ideals. "[He] will be found in camp ready as of old with genial welcome and well earned knowledge of woodcraft freely placed at the service of friends and his unwritten stories about the campfire, continue as of old, filled with quaint woodsy ideas and sounding like chapters taken bodily from the Arabian Nights. Long may the man and his Monument stand together."[32]

Helen Bartlett Bridgman wrote that "[Mr. Van] did valiantly declare, that, after the first shock and the lapse of time, his affections were again twining around the wreck of what once had been, and that he could honestly say it was as dear to him as ever. He said also that if he possessed a million dollars he would spend it all in planting trees, endeavoring to the utmost to restore to the world in every essential a spot without a rival in the whole Adirondack region."[33]

Many, many years later the land once pronounced by experts as the very finest square mile in all the Forest Preserve was restored. A new lodge was built and new trees grew beside the old sugar maples that protected the horses. Careful observers can still find fat old pine stumps that sit like charcoal ghosts, reminders of the fire of 1903.

Charred stumps, 1997.
Photo by author.

The Lake Placid Club
and Mr. Van

*. . .from time to time he would tell again the old Loj
campfire stories, usually around the big stone fireplace
in Forest Towers octagon.*

Godfrey Dewey, "The Adirondak Loj of Long Ago"

I N HIS LETTER to Lake Placid Club members about the fire destroy-
ing the Adirondack Lodge, Melvil Dewey wrote, "The old building was rapidly rotting and we can take our insurance and stand
the loss with composure....I wanted you to know promptly however
that bad as it is, it might have been much worse. 2 or 3 days later a
large force of men were to begin on Mrs. Dewey's new cottage and
the summer supplies would have been sent in with new furniture and
equipment, all of which would have been a total loss. The unexpected
delay...has resulted in saving some thousands of dollars."[1]

Melvil seemed sad about the loss of the lodge but also relieved to
be rid of the business headaches of the rotting log building. The
building was only twenty-five years old but, for aesthetic reasons the
bark had been left on the logs, and unfortunately, bark attracts insect
borers and retains dampness.

With the lodge gone, Melvil welcomed Mr. Van back to the Lake
Placid Club. In July, an agreement was signed: "V H will live at the
Club and be charged for board and rooms ½ the rate paid by Dewey

Mr. Van at Vanguard, Lake Placid Club, 1912.
Courtesy of Lake Placid Club Archives, Box SB-8D, Lake Placid Public Library.

and Gallup, also ½ list price for livery, laundry and boats. He will be electrical and mechanical expert and have supervision of motors, dynamos, pumps, automobiles and fire protection."[2] Mr. Van stayed at the little building that resided directly over the gasoline fire pump which in those days was an important safeguard. The place came to be called "Vanguard."

Mr. Van was not given a salary but was to record time worked and submit a bill. His bill would be audited and his account credited. He would be paid any balance after his expenses and charges at the club were satisfied.

The agreement was modified in August and totally rewritten in May of 1904. Apparently there had been accounting disagreements between Mr. Van and the finance people. The new agreement gave Mr. Van total freedom: "There are to be no slips or records of over time or discussion of any sort. It is left to Van to give an average of the 4 or 8 hours, as work may demand and his own convenience dictate." And it clearly stated how Melvil felt about Mr. Van: "He is to be treated as a member of the family, not as a mere employee."[3]

That agreement settled things for a while.

In 1904, Melvil Dewey decided to keep the Lake Placid Club open for a winter vacation. He opened the club amid snickers at the idea of going outdoors in the freezing cold. "Given the choice, who will go north instead of south in winter?" the scoffers asked.[4]

Ten hardy pioneers shared the first winter outing in Lake Placid: Henry Van Hoevenberg; Godfrey Dewey; Irving Bacheller, author; Anna Schultz Bacheller, his wife; Mrs. Ackerman; Dr. and Mrs. Edgar VanderVeer; Miss Wooster, her sister; Mrs. Ella B. Dana; and Ted (Edward C.) Dana, her son.

It was reported that "the ten skied, skated, tobogganed, snow-shoed, and otherwise gamboled in the snow, the women's petticoats sweeping the drifts. The experiment was a smashing success!"[5]

Godfrey Dewey recalled that "the first skis, which we brought to Lake Placid that first winter, were a curiosity. They were delivered with a single long pole and toe straps, and no one here, including myself, knew enough to know that they should have been equipped with harnesses."[6]

The next winter Melvil Dewey gathered a collection of skates and toboggans and welcomed over twenty guests. The event was repeated year after year with growing numbers of participants. Soon there was a new year-round clubhouse and outdoor teas, camp dinners, climbing, and even all-night camping parties. One participant noted: "Very few wallflowers or all-day sitters will you find in the winter colony....Here we are snowshoeing, skating and tobogganing at 10 below, warm as grizzly bears in full fur."[7]

In the winter evenings, Mr. Van entertained guests around the big open fire in the octagon room. One guest wrote: "And this will be one of the most appealing recollections of the Adirondack fortnight; the quiet kindliness in speech and manner of this old veteran of the forest, sitting in the flickering light of the log fire, dreaming aloud his visions of the days gone by."[8]

A group known as the Sno Birds was organized in 1920 and by 1922 had 500 members. The club had all the winter guests they could

**Curling on outdoor rink, very rarely attempted, before 1920.
Melvil Dewey in fur coat in front.**
Courtesy of Lake Placid Club Archives, Box SB-8, Lake Placid Public Library.

Winter pioneers of 1904. Seated (from left): unknown, Dr. Edgar Vanderveer, Mrs. Edgar Vanderveer, Standing (from left): Edward C. Dana, unknown, Godfrey Dewey with skis, Henry Van Hoevenberg in leather suit.

Courtesy of Lake Placid Club Archives, Box SB-8D, Lake Placid Public Library.

Winter group with toboggans, sleds, skis, and snowshoes, about 1909. Van Hoevenberg is second from left.

Courtesy of New York State Library.

care for and had to turn away many more. Even the Swiss confessed that "Placid has become the capital of winter sports."[9]

In February 1905, Mr. Van and Godfrey Dewey were staying at Lake Placid Club for the winter while Melvil and Mrs. Dewey were in Albany. Mr. Van wrote: "Things up here are running nicely. The house is still full, and there are more people coming—Dr. VanderVeer's father, and some others of his family. Godfrey is doing nicely, works in the pumphouse nearly every day. I am teaching him telegraphy, and we have a line run from his room to mine. He is learning very rapidly, and I think will be a fair operator by spring."[10]

Things might have been running nicely in Lake Placid but they were running very roughly in Albany. Melvil Dewey was in the middle of a fierce political battle. Dewey had just resigned from the Board of Regents over a quarrel about education unification. He continued as State Librarian and Director of the Library School, where he was accused of diverting too much of his attention to his club and spending too much time away from his office. Considerable testimony on behalf of Dewey squashed that accusation, but another, more serious, allegation followed.

A group of prominent citizens, headed by Louis Marshall, petitioned the Board of Regents for Dewey's resignation based on his practice of racial discrimination. Marshall, a successful New York lawyer, a defender of civil rights, and a prominent member of the Jewish community, objected to a public official of the State practicing the exclusion of Jews from his establishment, the Lake Placid Club.

The 1901 Club Handbook had stated: "No person is admitted as member or guest against whom there is any reasonable social, moral, race or physical objection."[11] This rule was intended to exclude consumptives, invalids, Jews, and blacks. It was an open display of discrimination but a practice common among establishments in the region at that time.

Dewey reasoned that since the establishment was a "club" and not a public hotel, the policy was legal and acceptable. Still, he was a public official. To this he argued that the membership policy was set by a council over which he personally had no control. Certainly, that argument was questionable.

On February 15, 1905, the Board of Regents condemned the publication of anti-Semitic expressions by an officer of the Education Department. They formally admonished Dewey's actions and stated "that the further control of a private business which continues to be conducted on such lines is incompatible with the legitimate requirements of his position."[12]

On September 21, Dewey resigned as State Librarian. He left behind the library, to which he had devoted many years of his life, and the University of the State of New York, to which he had made significant contributions. The Dewey family departed Albany and made the Lake Placid Club their year-round residence. Very quickly, Dewey's energies were redirected to expanding and improving the club.

Mr. Van kept busy at the club. Starting in 1909, he compiled weather data.[13] He also started the Adirondack Electric Co., cared for storage batteries, and worked on all sorts of small machinery. Mr. Van was always "working steadily at one hobby and another, always making himself useful in some way. He is a perfect wizard when it comes to machinery and he has a remarkable record in number of patents."[14]

During this period, Henry was granted six more patents: Combination Locking Device, Acetylene-Gas Lighter, Steeple-chase Puzzle, Gas-burner Cleaner, Protector for Telephone-Transmitters, and Photographic Apparatus. He also applied his ingenuity at the club. Long before there were thermostatic controls, he installed a "homemade electrical device in the Club Library which sounded a buzzer at the Front Desk on the floor below if temperature in the Library dropped below a certain level."[15]

Besides helping with machinery and electrical devices, Van Hoevenberg helped with entertainment at the club. "Here many members of the Club and others came to know and love him, and to enjoy the evenings when he would tell again around the fire blazing in some great stone fireplace the stories told round the old Lodge camp fires, or guide their searches of the heavens through his big telescope mounted on top of Forest Towers [a building at the club], or entertain them at Vanguard with the phonograph to which his ingenuity had added numerous refinements."[16]

Mr. Van also became interested in psychic phenomena, which had gained popularity and attracted the attention of the scientific world by the turn of the century. Godfrey Dewey recalled Mr. Van getting a group together to see if anything would happen. "What did happen were the kind of raps that are sometimes heard in such phenomena....The procedure is to ask questions and to get whatever phenomena there is to rap for yes or no. And I think it was the second time that we tried that Mr. Van suddenly discovered it was apparently in Morse code...It was unmistakably something like Morse code without a backstroke. About the second or third time the communicating control purported to be the famous Hank Bogardus."[17]

In his later years Mr. Van held private seances at the club. Several prominent psychic researchers attended, including I. K. Funk of Funk and Wagnalls and Professor James H. Hyslop of Columbia University. William James of Harvard also talked with Henry about psychic phenomena.[18]

Of course, Mr. Van dedicated most of his time to his genuine love—the woods. At some point, Henry longed for his old home and considered buying or leasing the lodge property from the Lake Placid Club. Melvil wrote: "We greatly wish to help you in your plans for the lodge. The cost to us stood $17,000 9 years ago, with interest $25,000 now. To any one but you we would not sell it...we will sell it to you for $6,000 or ¼ what it has cost us."[19]

As an alternative, Melvil offered Henry a ten-year lease. The details imply that Henry planned to spend a good deal of money rebuilding the lodge. Perhaps he had a financial backer since Melvil refers to "you and your associates." Unfortunately, an agreement was never reached and almost twenty years would pass before a new lodge was built.

Henry turned his efforts in another direction. In 1910, he became the first president of the Adirondack Camp and Trail Club (AC&TC). Once again "Mr. Van was to be found inspiring others to an understanding and love of the woods."[20] The membership consisted mostly of Lake Placid Club members and was largely devoted to trail work.

Henry Van Hoevenberg wrote: "Many parts of the Adirondacks are still practically inaccessible to all save the strongest and most hardy. Beautiful waterfalls, sublime mountain passes, grand ravines and the exquisite scenery of numerous points in this our country remain closed to nearly all who would appreciate them most, because of want of the small amount of attention the labor necessary to make them easily available involves. This work so ably and thoroughly done in the White Mountains by the Appalachian Club, has been totally neglected in the Adirondacks. It is to cover this deficiency that the Adirondack Camp and Trail Club has been organized."[21]

The goals of the AC&TC included cutting new trails, clearing out fallen trees and other debris each spring, building new camps, marking trails, organizing and conducting parties into the woods, arranging lectures on conservation, and teaching camp craft to young people and adults.[22] Many of these goals would be adopted by the Adirondack Mountain Club in the 1920s.

The first item on Mr. Van's list of projects was to re-open "the old trails that used to radiate from the Adirondack Lodge."[23] He asked for the Lake Placid Club's permission to build an open camp in the old maple forest on the south side of Heart Lake. The AC&TC also wanted to build a trail along the south shore from the outlet road to the camp and then continuing to the Indian Pass trail.

The Lake Placid Club granted permission and South Camp was probably constructed in 1911. Jim Goodwin remembers staying in that lean-to in 1922. It was later removed, but the South Camp trail is still used today.

The AC&TC work was thoroughly done and was appreciated by the growing number of campers and trampers. As an example of what members accomplished, in 1912 they cut thirty-five trees from the McIntyre trail; cut many fallen trees from other trails; completed a trail from Connery Pond to the Whiteface Mountain trail; built Sunrise Notch Camp and outfitted it with board floor, ruberoid roof, stone fireplace, table, benches, and cooking outfit; built a bridge at the great dam on the Indian Pass trail; put a new ruberoid roof on the Indian Pass camp; extended the Rocky Falls trail; and built two new bridges on that trail. All of this was done with a budget under $400.[24]

Although Henry was enthusiastic about his work with the AC&TC, financial problems seemed to be straining his relationship with the Lake Placid Club. In 1912, a letter from Melvil talks of money problems at the club: "It took last year $50,300 from Nov. 1 to July 1 above receipts to meet all our bills and these men who are furnishing money for the winter insist that we shall concentrate our work more on the summer months and reduce the burden every dollar we possibly can in the winter 6 months."[25]

Melvil told Henry that the Finance Committee had made several changes that would raise his room and board and cut his hours for two extra months in the winter. Melvil tried to smooth this over by promising to make up the room and board and assuring Henry that his summer salary would make up for the other two months. He must have expected Henry to be upset because he ends the letter with: "Now please don't get in your head that this means anything except as above. Things have been specially pleasant and there is the most friendly feeling for you on all sides and the only right thing to do is to fall in with the plan of the Committee...I know this is the best thing for you."[26]

Henry must have given in this time but there would be other spats because the Lake Placid Club repeatedly found itself in serious financial difficulties. Godfrey Dewey recalled: "For at least a third of a century, financial growing pains were our greatest problem. Melvil Dewey just could not bear to turn away, even at seasons of peak demand, those who would genuinely appreciate the Club's distinctive ideals and standards, and his willingness to spend next year's income year before last, if he could see a chance of getting it back thereafter, kept the Club in a chronically precarious financial condition, in spite of its unexampled prosperity."[27]

The next problem between Henry Van Hoevenberg and the club did not concern finances; it concerned spelling!

Melvil Dewey's passion for simplified spelling brought not only criticism but also laughs. Those unknowing thought his writings to be those of a second grader. About 1914, simplified spelling was applied at the club. Breakfast menus offered "slyst oranj, huni on tost, and cofi."

Van Hoevenberg never used simplified spelling (but he did drop the 'h' from the end of his name for some reason). In May 1914, Henry was upset about the spelling on a sign. He complained to Melvil:

A sign has been placed on the dock near this place, in which Vanguard is spelled "Vangard."

I object most decidedly to this. I accepted the name "Vanguard" and it has always been as my headquarters.

If you insist upon this, I must ask that some other name be given to the place, with which my own name is not connected.[28]

Simplified spelling had also been applied to Heart Lake, which became Hart Lake, and Adirondack Lodge, which became Adirondak Loj. However, "Hart" was hardly ever used. Even the club had abandoned simplified spelling by the 1950s. Godfrey scolded the club that "while organized efforts in fields away from the Club continues thru the Simpler Spelling Association, the Club's own disregard of the founder's principles and convictions puts the [Lake Placid Club Education] Foundation itself somewhat in the position of a bald-headed barber selling hair restorer."[29]

For some reason, "Adirondak Loj" stuck. It has been a frequent source of confusion but also a reminder of the origin of the new Loj.

Later in 1914, Henry was so unhappy about working arrangements that he submitted notice to terminate his agreement with the club. Melvil tried to help but Henry was persistent: "I have not at any time agreed to accept the cut of $400 in my salary."[30]

The club was having such tough times that there was nothing Melvil could do this time. He wrote (using simplified spelling): "I made veri clear that we wud all be veri glad to hav yu stay with us on much more liberal terms than any ov us hav but much az we shud regret to hav yu go, if yu think that iz wiser, we ar so tied up that we hav to submit to it."[31]

Letters from January 1915 show a tremendous strain between the two men. Henry was obviously very angry and bitter while Melvil was doing his best to smooth things over, but his hands were tied as far as finances were concerned. He wrote to Henry, "Think twice before yu cut yurself off from yur old home."[32]

Somehow, things were patched up and an agreement was signed on April 15. Two years later trouble started again and this time the ending was different. Henry terminated the agreement and Melvil did not try to stop him: "It won't seem natural at the Club not to see yu about and I hope yur new venture is in Placid so that we shal see yu often and keep up the frendship of the last 16 years. We always think of yu as one of the family."[33] He also said that the only reason the club kept Vanguard running was because Mr. Van had been there so long. Now that he had volunteered to go they would close up Vanguard.

In May 1917, Mr. Van moved across Mirror Lake to expand his Adirondack Electric Co. The *Lake Placid News* reported: "Henry Van Hoevenberg has left the club and transferred his business to this side of the lake. Quartered in the Noble block he will repair safe locks, typewriters, phonographs, sewing machines, spark cells, and treat storage batteries scientifically. He will continue to keep his boat Cynthia for taking parties around the lake."[34]

At the rear of Noble block, Henry occupied rooms and built a new boathouse for his electric launch, Cynthia. It must have been an unusual boat because fifty years later Kenneth Bliss, a Lake Placid native who was associated with the marina of George and Bliss, remembered "the old electric boat on Mirror Lake was owned by Van Hoevenberg. He operated it as a ferry on the lake."[35]

Mr. Van seems to have been a popular and respected citizen of Lake Placid. A news article of 1917 described him as a "well-known machinist, electrician, boatman, guide, author, president of the Adirondack Camp and Trail Club, and all-round genial gentleman."[36]

On Sunday, February 17, 1918, Henry started on a short hike and was seized with a severe pain in the chest. Like a true tramper, he walked home with some assistance. He was taken to the Lake Placid Club, where he slowly regained his strength. On Monday, February 25, "he was seized with another attack and died suddenly and quietly about noon."[37] The death certificate officially reports he died at 11 a.m. on Feb. 25. It lists Cause of Death as Angina Pectoris and a Contributory Factor as Chronic Endocarditis, which had lasted five years.[38]

Services were held at Lake Placid the following afternoon. In a tribute, Godfrey Dewey wrote: "Mr. Van was a wonderful Character...endowed with inventive genius....He will always remain as genial guide, inspiring philosopher and true friend.

"With the passing of Mr. van Hoevenberg breaks the last living link connecting the Adirondacks of today with the first pioneer days of the past; but his spirit lives in the heart and memory of hundreds and thousands who owe gratefully to him their love of nature and the woods; and the spirit of Adirondack Lodge, his spirit in a body drawn from the woods he loved, shall stand for all time his eternal monument in the heart of the everlasting hills."[39]

The matter of Henry Van Hoevenberg's estate was settled in Surrogate's Court in Essex County. Gertrude C. Knight, his sister and sole heir, petitioned the court. The petition stated the value of Van Hoevenberg's personal property was less than four hundred dollars. He held no real estate, left no widow heir surviving, and left no will, except an old one as described in the affidavit of Gertrude's husband, Joseph Knight.[40]

Knight wrote to several people who knew Henry and tried to find the whereabouts of the witnesses to Henry's will. He found that they were both dead. He was unable to find any people who could swear to the handwriting of the witnesses; thus there was no way to prove the will from 1880 was legitimate.

Since there was no recent will to indicate Henry's wishes, Gertrude sent Henry's body to Troy to be buried in the family lot in Oakwood Cemetery. Henry's body and most of his possessions were gone from the Adirondacks. It was later rumored that one of his leather suits hung in a Lake Placid store window. The famous leather visor cap found its way to the Adirondack Museum in Blue Mountain Lake.

Although Henry was gone from the mountains, he was not forgotten. The work of the Adirondack Camp and Trail Club carried on. In preparation for the 1932 Olympic Winter Games, South Mountain was renamed Mount Van Hoevenberg. Soon, another effort was under way to pay tribute to Van Hoevenberg: "Shortly after Mr. Van's death, a group of friends proposed a memorial to him and to the original Adirondak Loj in the form of a bronze tablet to be mounted on the Eagle's Claw rock... It is not a utilitarian project and there are many more pressing needs for funds to develop the present Loj, but at some future time it would be most fitting if this proposal could be carried thru."[41]

In the fall of 1968, fifty years after the death of Henry Van Hoevenberg, the Adirondack Mountain Club placed a memorial plaque on Eagle's Claw Rock. The rock sits beside the site of the original lodge and near the original start of the Van Hoevenberg trail to Marcy. The trail has been moved but the rock and the plaque have not. They continue to celebrate Henry's legacy.

HENRY VAN HOEVENBERG
22 MARCH 1849—25 FEB 1918

ADIRONDAK LOJ
1878-1903

JUST NORTH OF THIS SPOT BESIDE THE LAKE CHOSEN FROM THE SUMMIT OF TAHAWUS AS THE VERY HEART OF THE ADIRONDACKS HENRY VAN HOEVEN-BERG CREATED THE ORIGINAL ADIRONDAK LOJ—AN IMPOSING LOG STRUCTURE BUILT OF VIRGIN TIMBER CUT ON THE SITE. "MR. VAN" BUILT ALSO THE PRIN-CIPAL TRAILS RADIATING FROM HERE AND PIO-NEERED THE OPENING OF THE ADIRONDAKS TO ALL WILDERNESS LOVERS UNTIL THE LÒJ WAS DE-STROYED BY THE LAST GREAT FOREST FIRES OF 1903.

ADIRONDAK LOJ AND ITS FOUNDER ARE GONE BUT HERE IN THE HEART OF THE ETERNAL HILLS THEIR SPIRIT LIVES TO INSPIRE FOREVER ALL LOVERS OF THE WOODS.

ERECTED 1968

The great Lake Placid Club and its founder have gone the way of Henry and his lodge. Melvil Dewey died at his "Lake Placid Club" in Florida on December 26, 1931, at the age of 80. Godfrey Dewey died at Placid Memorial Hospital on October 19, 1977, at the age of 90. By then the original club in Lake Placid, New York, had gone downhill and could no longer survive as a private entity. After reorganizations and defaults on mortgages, it was sold in November of 1980 to Massanutten Corp. Other sales and foreclosures followed. In the end there were auctions and fires. Only a few buildings survive today.

Regardless of the club's discrimination policies, the Deweys and the Lake Placid Club should be remembered for their accomplishments regarding the Heart Lake property: promoting the AC&TC, building a new lodge, leasing and then selling the property to good stewards, supporting the Adirondack Mountain Club, and naming Mount Van Hoevenberg.

Photo by author.

The New Adirondak Loj

The Lodge is dead. Long live the Lodge!

Melvil Dewey

SHORTLY AFTER THE FIRE OF 1903 destroyed Adirondack Lodge, Melvil Dewey notified Lake Placid Club members that "as fast as possible at any reasonable cost the blackened surface will be covered again with foliage, new trees started and a new Lodge spring up on the shores of what was meant for the most attractive spot in all the great wilderness...Keep a warm place in your heart for the home in the forest of which we were all so fond, and before long we shall meet again on the shores of the little lake in the Heart of the Adirondacks. The Lodge is dead. Long live the Lodge!"[1]

During the summer of 1903, club members and visitors were entertained in camps on the shore of Heart Lake. As the months went by, the expense and difficulty of building a new lodge must have been realized because the only structure built near the site was a lumber camp.

Harold Howland and Arthur Hewitt snowshoed from Lake Henderson through Indian Pass toward the lumber camp in 1905. Howland wrote, "Our path now lay across land scarred and slashed by the lumberman's ax. There was no beauty to divert us.... . It seems ages that we plodded along that gloomy road, passing a couple of deserted lumber camps, crossing Clear Lake, turning beyond into an old tote road, long untraveled."[2] They found the group of buildings just beyond the lake. Inside the shanty, they sat in a large, low-raftered room, lighted by lanterns and heated by a stove in the middle. The men warmed themselves, ate the supper offered by the shanty boss, and slept soundly in their bunks.

By 1908, the Lake Placid Club handbook stated (in simplified spelling): "The great forest fire of 1903, which destroyd the Lodge and its 16 subsidiary bildings, fortunately spared most of the trails and scenery which made the Lodge famous. A temporary lodge and a stable with 6 stalls have been bilt, and a 100 acre island of safety cleard, so that the rebilt Lodge will be safe from forest fires."

That was great public relations talk. The scenery near Indian Pass held "no beauty" according to Howland. The club's "100 acre island of safety cleard" really meant the property was being logged. The charred debris was hauled away, sound dead timber was turned into charcoal, and any valuable standing trees were cut for lumber.[3] Howland wrote: "Along the banks of a little stream that looked as if half a dozen logs would choke it were piled cord after cord of the raw material from which newspapers were made. The little stream in a few months would sweep those logs away like toothpicks and carry them down to their destination."[4]

The promise to rebuild the lodge was not being fulfilled either. The temporary house could accommodate only a few mountain climbers for a night or two. It certainly did not appease those who remembered the original lodge. "The former thick woods were annihilated—not a tree left to tell the tale," wrote one. "A camp, of bare unpainted lumber, erected since the fire, for the convenience of stray pedestrians, only emphasized the misery on every side. The stone foundation and a wrecked chimney indicated where the Lodge had been. Yet the old wooden curb of the well had outlived that night, as well as the persistent evergreen which used to climb over and follow a great flat rock close to the dining room for the nourishment it sought and found. It is the homely details that tug so at your heartstrings, and that unburnt curb, with the familiar roots beside it twining about the rock still, brought the tears to my eyes."[5]

For others, like T. Morris Longstreth, the spot still held tremendous charm.

It is easy to believe that Heart Pond before the forest fire was the supreme gem of the wilderness. The slopes of the great mountains rise on all sides. Only an unmarred forest is wanting to complete the picture of sheltered loveliness....Heart Pond, formerly known as Clear Pond, fulfilled our most exacting tastes, and we set about settling for an indefinite stay...

It was going to be a cold night....We had found a shack with a stove in it. The shack was made of boards and designed for comfort in a Texas summer. The boards kept out the larger masses of air that beat upon the house, but the cracks, which made the wall look very much like a paling fence laid on its side, let in narrow strips of cold. The result gave you the effect of sitting in forty draughts at once. Lynn said that he didn't like his cold striped.[6]

Toward the end of his trip, Longstreth reflected on his stay at the pond:

The first thought instigated by the more enchanting places in the Park was to settle in each one for life. Since that proved inconvenient offhand, the next was to promise ourselves an immediate return for that purpose. Consequently there are at least half a dozen localities where we are engaged to spend the rest of our days. Heart Pond is one of these. Not right in that shack, understand, but at a little distance where angels come, but do not trouble the water in order not to frighten the trout.[7]

Recovery at Heart Lake progressed slowly. Grasses, berry bushes, and shrubs had grown in the open spaces after the fire. Then fire cherry, quaking aspen, and birch were flourishing with a few red maple and black cherry taking root.

In 1923, the reorganized Camp and Trail Club of the Lake Placid Club announced its plans for Heart Lake: keep Jed Rossman as caretaker from May 5 until late October, stock the lake with fish and close it for two years, collect a fund for reforesting the area, and build a new shelter on the east shore of the lake for club guests.[8]

To speed the recovery of the forest, acres of red and white pine were planted by Harry Hicks, Jed Rossman, and others. The plantings started at the bridge over Marcy Brook and continued along the road to Heart Lake and then farther south. The one-year transplants

Facing page: Pines planted in 1920s.
Photo by author.

from the state nursery near Paul Smith's cost five dollars per thousand.[9]

Jim Goodwin remembers those years: "I knew the Loj area in the 1920s where colorful Jed Rossman lived in a cabin, and rented lean-tos to non-Lake Placid Club members if no member wanted one. The woods consisted of small birch and poplar except where the Club had planted hundreds of red pine. There were still open fields offering good blue-berrying in season. Trails, mostly using the newly built wood roads, led up Marcy, Algonquin, and Jo as well as to Indian and Avalanche Passes."[10]

In February 1922, Ed Leggett reported, "One of the highlights of my week at the [Lake Placid] Club was a day's outing by sleigh at Heart Lake…One morning about twelve of us piled into a big box sleigh filled with straw and blankets. It was pulled by two horses, and after a ride of about two hours we arrived at Heart Lake."[11]

Another winter day, in early 1927, Harry Wade Hicks, secretary of the Lake Placid Club, made the same trip. He spent the night with Jed Rossman in his shack at the lake and the next morning walked to the center of the ice-covered lake to watch the sunrise. As he stood on Heart Lake he was inspired by "a scene of matchless beauty, especially as the pink color of the sunrise flooded the peaks of Marcy and the several peaks of the MacIntyre Range."[12] He conceived a plan to rebuild Adirondack Lodge.

**Harry Hicks in suit, Jed Rossman, and Joe Bernier
in field by Heart Lake, about 1922.**
Courtesy of Adirondack Mountain Club.

Hicks' conviction grew as the sun rose. Then he heard the breakfast horn and Jed's loud lumberjack call, "Grub's ready; come and git it." Hicks walked to the old lodge site and again heard "Grub's ready; come and git it." Hicks did not want food; he asked Jed for a pencil and paper. At the end of twenty minutes Hicks had captured the inspiration on paper. He had written a letter to individuals who might be able to contribute to a building fund.[13]

The Lake Placid Club approved Hicks' plan to build a lodge and the letter of appeal went out exactly as written that day at Heart Lake.

Ever since the Adirondack Lodge had burned, the Lake Placid Club had been promising to replace it. It seemed the time had finally come. Perhaps time had healed the sadness of Henry's death. Perhaps the ferns and aspens and fire cherry were covering the deep scars in the woods. And, with the newly formed Adirondack Mountain Club taking responsibility for the majority of trail and shelter work, the Camp and Trail Club was free to direct money and energy to the Heart Lake property.

Plans for a new lodge moved forward with funds coming from members of the Camp and Trail Club and Sno Birds organizations of the Lake Placid Club. When the campaign came to a standstill, Henry Stetson supplied the $9,000 needed to meet the goal.

The Saranac Lake architect William G. Distin worked on plans for a new lodge. Distin had designed several of the Lake Placid Club buildings and understood the enormous task of trying to replace the famous Adirondack Lodge. His father, a professional photographer, had photographed the illustrious structure and grounds. As a young lad, William had himself visited the original lodge just a week before it burned in 1903.

Distin began his career with William Coulter, whose architectural firm brought national attention to the rustic design. "He [Distin] was the last of an unbroken line of Great Camp designers, using elemental wood and stone to capture a unique regional style," says Mary B. Hotaling.[14]

Distin's design for the lodge was characteristic of his style. To make the building resemble log construction, he used horizontal boards and projecting squared-off logs. The upper level had Swiss-style cutouts. The interior employed rustic features including a large stone fireplace. Although the new lodge would be smaller and simpler

Loj Living Room.
Courtesy of Ken and Nancy Foster.

Adirondak Loj, about 1945.
Courtesy of Ken and Nancy Foster.

than the original lodge, Distin captured the woodsy and comfortable spirit always present at Heart Lake.

Construction began in the spring of 1927. In June, the club reported: "The new all-year camp at Adirondak loj has been started. Funds hav been secured, plans approved and the camp will be redy for use in October." In November, the club announced that the new all-year camp was completed, "except for several much-needed features necessarily omitted because capital specially provided was insufficient." They needed at least $3,000 for furnishings and equipment. By completion, the camp cost over $30,000.[15]

The new lodge, located in the clearing just north of the original site, welcomed its first guests on December 26, 1927.[16] Twenty-four years after the fire destroyed the original Adirondack Lodge, a new lodge was open, "largely restoring to its former glory one of America's most attractive tramping and camping centers."[17] Dewey had made good on his promise to resurrect the lodge. Long live the Lodge!

Now, however, Dewey used simplified spelling, so the camp was named "Adirondak Loj" and Heart Lake was "Hart Lake." The Loj featured two bunkrooms and four private rooms. The large living room served duty as a dining room and had a loft for overflow guest quarters. Outside the main lodge were an electric light plant, stable, ice house, and pure water. "Hart lake is absolutely pure," promised the Loj brochure.

One guest commented, "Furnace heat, electric lights, unlimited hot water, shower baths, a commodious drying room for wet clothing, good bunk rooms with comfortable bunks, a spacious fireplace and plenty of lounging chairs, and plain but delicious meals, all contribute to the attraction of this ideal climbing center, adapted for every season of the year."[18] Another remarked, "The happy but tired skier is glad to join the circle about the huge fireplace, and to let the warmth of the flames and the soothing crackle of the logs relax his taut muscles and lend color to his story of the day's adventure."[19]

Mr. and Mrs. Richard Ashe were the first caretakers. Prices for club members were:

Single Bunk	$1.00
Breakfast 7:30-8:00	$1.00
Dinner 12:30-1:30	$1.50
Supper 6:00-7:00	$1.50

Rooms and meals were available only to Lake Placid Club members or those guests introduced by club members. Non-member guests paid twenty percent more. As practiced by Van Hoevenberg, "meals wil be servd in camp style with emfasis on good cooking but without frils,"[20] noted a club brochure. Since the Loj was a part of the Lake Placid Club, its rules and standards were applied. Liquor, gambling, profanity, and all smoking by women were prohibited. Simplified spelling was encouraged.

The cozy and comfortable living room looked remarkably as it still looks today. Paintings, pictures, and heads of wild game adorned the walls. A moose head now rests where an elk head projected and the mountain goat head, white goose, and duck are gone. Hickory chairs and settee and yellow birch chandeliers still adorn the woodsy room. The lights have always gone off at ten o'clock.

Back then there were no co-ed facilities. There were separate bunkrooms and separate bathing and toilet facilities. The women's bunkroom faced the lake and had patterned bed covers, a braided rug, and floral window shades. The men's bunkroom looked out at the outbuildings and enjoyed the noise of the generator.

The club allowed the public to use camp sites, fireplaces, and three of the sleeping shelters. "From time immemorial Algonquin and Iroquois indians, lumbermen, hunters and trappers, sientists and now modern sportsmen hav used the Loj site as a camping center. It wil always be preservd by Club for this purpose."[21]

Overnight in a shelter cost fifty cents per person; tent sites cost twenty-five cents per person. Proper camping etiquette was encouraged: "Every Adirondak camper should be a true conservationist." The brochure asked campers to use only fireplaces for cooking sites, to burn all garbage, and to leave a little dry wood in the shelter for the next camper. Some vandals must have prompted the request that campers not shoot or burn or injure signs. They were also asked to cut only dead or fallen trees for fire and to protect even the smallest young trees.

The new lodge met with immediate success. Among the first guests were Arthur Hopkins of the state Conservation Department, Thomas Gilchrist, Alexander Miller, Robert Carter, and Russell Carson. The party spent Lincoln's Birthday weekend at the new

Adirondak Loj. From the Lake Placid Club they rode in an old-fashioned three-seater sleigh over the twelve miles to the lodge. They reported: "The blazing log fire and the hot supper awaiting made a splendid ending to a cold ride. Adirondack Lodge is the last word in roughing it easy."[22]

In May 1928, the club reported "Adirondak Loj did a rushing business while several winter mountain climbing parties set out from there. The rejister at the loj bears interesting record of trips that different groups took."[23] By March of 1929, "Adirondak loj was so popular this winter that it was crowded to capacity more than once...One woman brought a house party of 13 and entertaind them at the loj. More and more this all-year camp is coming into its ryt."[24]

Evidently the Depression years reduced the use of the Adirondak Loj by Lake Placid Club members. The club was in financial trouble once again and decided to sell some property in the spring of 1932. Perhaps if Melvil Dewey had still been alive he could have pulled the club through its troubles. Unfortunately, without Melvil there to help, the desirable property was put up for sale and rumored to be attracting offers from persons interested in making it a speakeasy.[25]

Frederick T. Kelsey, a Governor of the new Adirondack Mountain Club and a member of the Lake Placid Club, put a stop to that. He organized the Adirondak Loj Corporation and negotiated a long-term lease of the new lodge. He personally paid the lease and expenses of the Loj.

Kelsey envisioned a much wider and broader use of the Loj. He opened the property to the general public, eliminated simplified spelling (except for Adirondak Loj), lowered the cost of meals, and promoted the recreational and conservation aims of the Adirondack Mountain Club.

The facility was now open to all campers, trampers, sportsmen, sportswomen, and vacationers. The Adirondak Loj brochure reiterated the creed of all those who visit Heart Lake: "For those who love the North woods, the Loj situated at the foot of the highest Adirondack peaks, in a setting not surpassed for beauty, presents an ideal camp de-luxe. Fresh air, good fellowship, glorious hikes and climbs, and comfort and good comradeship at night about the fireplace combine to make it unique. Adirondak Loj is at the end of the road and the beginning of the trampers' and skiers' paradise."

The Adirondack Mountain Club

Truly, if one wants to know what ADK is all about, a visit to Heart Lake will quickly show it.

Bruce Wadsworth, *With Wilderness at Heart*

ALTHOUGH CLUBS like the Adirondack Camp and Trail Club and the Adirondack Trail Improvement Society were working hard at improving trails and shelters, they were somewhat exclusive in membership and limited in the region they covered. An Adirondack club was needed—a club for *everyone* who loved the outdoors.

The Adirondack Mountain Club (later known as ADK) was incorporated on April 23, 1922. Its 208 charter members included Franklin D. Roosevelt, Gifford Pinchot, Dr. Irving Langmuir, Louis Agassiz Fuertes, Jane Rippin, Harry Wade Hicks, T. Morris Longstreth, Alfred Donaldson, and rivals Melvil Dewey and Louis Marshall.

William G. Howard of the Conservation Commission gave a speech at the organization meeting outlining the usefulness of the new club. He felt it would stimulate interest in hiking and climbing among sports-minded persons and would increase the pleasure of those already enjoying the mountains by opening new trails and creating new camps. He also felt the club could improve the careless camping manners of campers and sportsmen by pledging to adhere to high ethics of conservation and sportsmanship. These ideals sound very similar to the ideals spoken by Henry Van Hoevenberg at the founding of the Adirondack Camp and Trail Club (which became Camp and Trail Club to avoid confusion with Adirondack Mountain Club).

One of the first projects the club undertook was acquiring land in the Johns Brook Valley and building John Brooks Lodge. This created a central hiking base in the Adirondack high peaks and made ADK the connecting link between the Ausable Club in the east and the Lake Placid Club in the west. Once John Brooks Lodge opened in 1925, new trails were quickly cleared to create a network across the entire high peaks region.

ADK quickly gained recognition as a distinguished organization. In 1928, Walter O'Kane wrote: "It is of course by its accomplishments in the mountains that the influence and value of the club are to be judged. These have been noteworthy."[1] For a complete history of the Adirondack Mountain Club, see *With Wilderness at Heart* by Bruce Wadsworth.

In the spring of 1932, Frederick T. Kelsey started ADK's association with the Heart Lake property. He organized the Adirondak Loj Corporation and negotiated with the Lake Placid Club (of which he was a prominent member) for a long-term lease of the lodge.

Mr. Kelsey paid the lease and handled all the finances but opened the property to the general public and promoted the aims of the Adirondack Mountain Club. For twenty-five years, the Loj would be used extensively by ADK members thanks to the kindness of Mr. Kelsey.

Orville and Nellie Cobane were put in charge of the Loj and Jed Rossman took care of the shelters, camp sites, and supplies. Orville had worked for the Lake Placid Club and thus was a key player in keeping the close connection that existed between the two organizations at that time. He quickly caught on to the spirit of the lodge; he often explained how the moose head got on the parlor wall. "Well, I'll tell you," he said. "We chased that moose in the back door, through the kitchen. He was going so fast he jammed his head right through the wall into the living room. And then we sawed off the rest and left the head there."[2]

Jed spent many years at the Loj taking care of visitors, telling stories, chewing tobacco, sitting on the fence, and playing cards. One famous night, Mrs. Rossman argued with Jed until he was so mad he yelled "Go to hell!" He flew out the door and headed for his cabin at the Loj. Later that night, as Jed was finishing a poker game at his cabin, Mrs. Rossman burst through the door. She smiled and said, "You told me to go to hell and so here I am."[3]

Jed's portrait still hangs on the living room wall at the Loj.

Through the 1930s and '40s winter facilities and activities expanded greatly and the Loj remained open until mid-March or even early April. The Rimrock slope and the Nye Ski Trail started being used in 1932 for practice for the Winter Olympics. The first Loj Ski School was held in January 1938 and was led by Otto Schneibs.

A Loj brochure proclaimed: "From the shimmering spruce-girt mountains encircling the Loj there drop some of the best-known ski runs and tours in the East. A smooth and delightfully varied practice slope and slalom glade is reserved for the exclusive use of Loj guests. So is the wide, curving Rimrock Run, dropping 810 feet in 9/16 mile, a miniature 'Nose Dive' used for Class C time trials." The skier could also find Wright Peak Run with a drop of 2,300 feet, Whale's Tail Run, and the Mount Marcy Trail. Mountaineers could head to snowy Avalanche Lake.

An ADK Bulletin reported: "The Loj road will be well-plowed. New books will be added to the small library. The new lighting system will make the long evenings still more enjoyable. All touring trails have been mowed. Rimrock has been manicured. The ski tow will multiply the pleasures of mornings and afternoons on the practice slope. Dull cares of the city will be forgotten. So plan the trip, get out from storage the dusty skis, buy some fresh wax, shake out the parka, oil the boots, and write Mary for a reservation."[4]

Reportedly, the Loj always lost money in the winter, but the loss was less than the cost of a caretaker, so the Loj remained open. Loyal guests braved frigid, frosty nights in the bunkroom in exchange for a few hours of marvelous mountain skiing.[5]

In the winter of 1941, the Cobanes offered a spring skiing package. Skiers could express their skis five days in advance and Orville would have them toted up Mount Marcy. For $5, they would

Skiers at Adirondak Loj with Mount Jo in background, 1944. Notice the lack of spruce and fir on Mount Jo forty years after the fire.
Courtesy of Ken and Nancy Foster.

Aerial view, April 1947: Rimrock ski slope (1), Loj ski slope (2), Whale's Tail (3), to Mount Marcy (4), to Avalanche Pass (5).
USGS

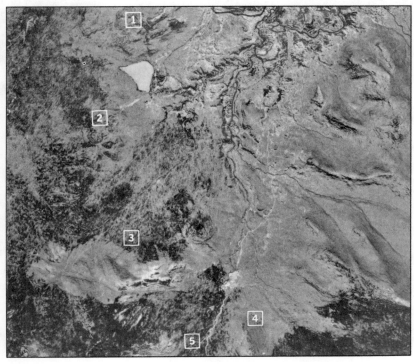

tote up blankets and skis, have a guide cook meals at Plateau Lean-to on Saturday and Sunday, and provide Sunday dinner at the Loj.[6]

The Cobanes left after ten years (perhaps that winter of 1941 tired them out) and the Gebos arrived in 1942. An ADK Bulletin from 1945 reports: "Mr. and Mrs. Dominic Gebo (Nick and Mary) happily remain in charge. They have survived the winter splendidly and both are in the best of spirits. Nick is at present trapping suckers in Heart Lake so to eliminate the chief enemy of the trout."[7]

New hosts, Joe and Myrtle Trapasso, took over in 1946. They not only took care of the guests but adopted a fawn as well. In early spring, a game warden found a four-day old fawn and carried her to the Loj, where Myrtle took her in and fed her by bottle until she was able to eat on her own. By December, "Beauty" had lost her spots and stood 30 inches tall thanks to the care of Myrtle and all the Loj guests that summer.[8]

In 1946, Harry Wade Hicks sent letters to Loj guests encouraging them to become ADK members and to continue to patronize the Heart Lake facility. "The Loj is a grand place," he wrote. "The undersigned visited it first in 1896, when Henry Van Hoevenberg was wont to regale his guests with marvelous stories of the Wilderness. It is our ambition to perpetuate his spirit, and his love for all that then entered into, and still distinguishes, what we call 'The Wilderness.' "

Room and meal rates for ADK members had barely changed from the rates of the 1930s:[9]

Bunk	$1.50
Breakfast	$1.00
Luncheon	$1.35
Supper	$1.65
Leantos per night	$0.50 per person

In the summer, the Trading Post offered camping supplies and Heart Lake now had a boathouse, canoes, a rowboat, a diving float, and bath houses. By this time, the Loj had started charging twenty-five cents a day for parking for those not registered at the Loj. The only road on the property was a loop west toward Heart Lake past the Loj, then south along the lake (this stretch is now a grassy walkway), and then back west through the open campsite area and around to the entry point.[10]

About this time, Harry Hicks wrote: "The importance of the Loj as a center to encourage mountaineering is illustrated by the fact that on some days, at one time, twenty or more cars are parked in the open space adjacent to the Loj."[11] What would he think of the current 200 or more cars per day?

Life at the Loj was primitive, but lovers of the woods relished their visits: "People live close together. Hence bunkroom space involves no apology...Members do not look for luxury as in a hotel. Waiting for a chance to get into the tub or under the shower after exercise involves no serious hardship. It is only important that all present make concessions to the common comfort and to fraternize as true devotees of the wilderness do when on the trail."[12]

When Kelsey died suddenly in 1957, the Lake Placid Club decided to sell the property rather than continue to lease it. It wanted to sell to the state or to some non-profit organization that would care for the property. This was Godfrey Dewey's second great tribute to Henry Van Hoevenberg—preservation of this fine square mile of property.

Dewey offered the Loj to ADK for just $35,000. Even though it was a very reasonable price, the purchase would be a great undertaking for the Adirondack Mountain Club, with just over 2,000 members, little money, and no lodge management experience. Members responded, "Oh, we cannot let it go!"[13]

The ADK Board of Governors voted to approve the purchase because the property seemed an ideal location for members and others wanting to go hiking, climbing, camping, and fishing in the high peaks area. The Board "felt that the club would be materially strengthened in what it could offer its members and that it would become a focal point for the conservation program and eventually become its central headquarters."[14]

Of course, it became much of that and more. In 1997, Bruce Wadsworth wrote, "Perhaps nothing else of Club interest so integrates the recreation, education and conservation goals of ADK than the combined programs that have emanated from this property.

Truly, if one wants to know what ADK is all about, a visit to Heart Lake will quickly show it."[15]

ADK leased the property until April 1, 1959, when it purchased the Loj and the 640-acre tract (actually, it turned out to be 704 acres). ADK paid a $10,000 down payment and mortgaged the rest. The club also paid the Kelsey estate $6,750 for the truck, generator, furniture, linens, and other personal items on the property.

Evidently, Godfrey Dewey, then vice-president of Lake Placid Club Stores, Inc., wanted to guarantee that the Loj property would be preserved and used as he deemed proper. Thus, the deed contained two unusual restrictions:

A. That the party of the second part (Adirondack Mountain Club, Inc.) will not sell or lease the said premises, or any part thereof, to any person, firm, corporation (except the State of New York, to become part of the Forest Preserve of said State) without written consent of the party of the first part.

B. That the party of the second part, or its grantees or lessees, will not conduct, or permit to be conducted, upon said premises, the sale of intoxicating liquors.[16]

The story of the fund drive conducted to finance the purchase was well told by ADK's president at the time, A. Ranger Tyler, in an article in ADK's magazine, *Adirondac*, aptly titled "Fund Collecting: Its Perils and Joys or How to Buy a Loj in Three Hectic Years." He described how the checks and coins and crumbled dollar bills and stock certificates poured in and how he visited the bank 270 times to make deposits and withdrawals.[17]

The club was able to pay off the entire mortgage in three years instead of five. By 1962, the club owned the Loj, lock, stock and bunkrooms, and was briefly out of debt. There was already talk of the need for improved Loj facilities.

The Loj building was thirty-five years old. Originally designed to accommodate twenty-four guests and a staff of two, it now welcomed forty guests and had a staff of seven at busy times. Adequate toilet rooms were needed for the growing number of guests. Living quarters needed to be expanded for the staff. Camping facilities also needed improvements to handle the eighty people who might be there in the summer. In those days, campers were kept away from the Loj area, a policy probably carried over from the Lake Placid Club ownership period. In 1962 the campers were built a new washhouse with flush toilets, a new dock, and ten picnic tables.

In 1963, William G. Distin, the original architect of the Loj, designed two additions to the Loj building: a new wing with toilet facilities and a twenty-foot extension of the existing kitchen wing to house a new kitchen and living quarters for the staff. The existing first-floor bunkrooms were walled off into smaller "family" bunkrooms and the old kitchen and staff area became a new dining room. The living room was far more comfortable and spacious without the dining furniture in it. The biggest change was probably the new bathrooms with multiple toilets, showers, and wash basins. "The Club now has a Loj of which it can be proud,"[18] wrote one guest.

There were also improvements in heating units, water lines, electric wiring, and the generator. ADK was discovering the difficulty of running a year-round lodge in the wilderness. It was hoped that the improvements would reduce maintenance costs and prevent frequent and costly emergencies.

Ken and Nancy Foster remember what it was like being caretakers at the Loj in 1965. "We had the generator our first year. We were on the stand-by generator all summer. It gave us enough power to run one freezer, the water pump and one electrical outlet in the kitchen. The guests thought it was great. They loved the atmosphere. Boy!"[19]

In 1967, when the new local supplier of electrical service quoted a reasonable rate, ADK put in a power line. Still, with installation and other charges, the cost for the line was over $15,000. ADK kept the Loj generator to use for emergencies. When Lake Placid lost power and was dark, the Loj was bright as day.

The Fosters were more than just caretakers of the Loj. They really cared for the people, too. It was not an easy job being cook, plumber, host, carpenter, dishwasher, housekeeper, and more. But the Fosters also kept an eye on their guests. They found out where they were going and when they expected to be back. They even started cold cars in the winter while the owners were away snow camping.[20]

Ken Foster helped build the nature museum that stood behind the Loj. A testament to Ken's carpentry work is that when the

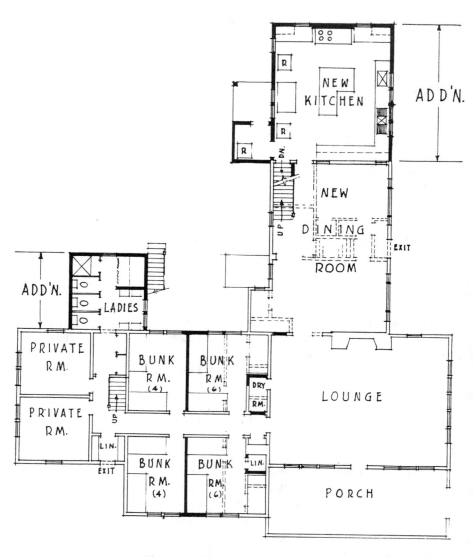

· FIRST FLOOR PLAN ·

**Drawings of Loj additions
by Acton R. Davies, 1963.**
  Courtesy of *Adirondac.*

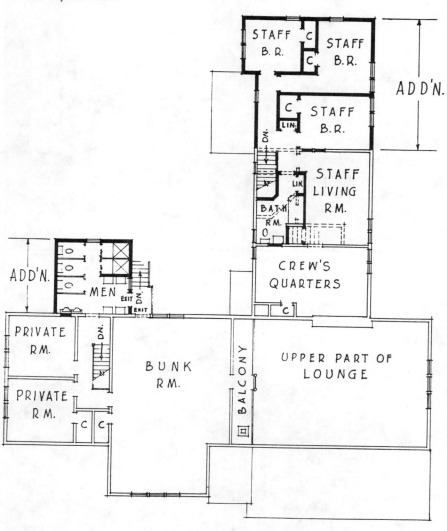

· SECOND FLOOR PLAN ·

museum was moved a few years ago it was lifted up, rolled down the lake path, and set on a new foundation, still superbly intact.

Another builder was always there to help ADK raise money. Adolph "Ditt" Dittmar became known as "The Man Who Built Picnic Tables." Ditt also helped build huge benches at the amphitheater.

Numerous buildings have come and gone over the years. The stable, the caretakers' cottage, the trading post, the bunkhouse, Chipmunks' Retreat, and the ice house are gone. A special building was added in 1973. It cemented ADK's role as steward, educator, and guide in the High Peaks region. ADK built the Campers and Hikers Building (now called the High Peaks Information Center) to accommodate the needs of the growing number of hikers. It includes an assembly porch, meeting room with a capacity of up to a hundred persons, Trading Post, public toilets, pay showers, and staff housing. A unique feature of the building is the fireplace, a memorial to former ADK President Borden Mills. It contains specimens of rocks native to the Adirondacks.

Although the number of visitors was increasing and the Loj had many loyal guests, the facility still lost money most years. About 1980, things began to turn around when a new emphasis on hospitality was encouraged among the staff.

Some promoters want to do more—perhaps television and telephones, private baths and jacuzzis would attract more guests. But those who come back year after year resist changes; it is a treat to submerge oneself into the peaceful lifestyle of early ADKers.

One member reports staying in a lean-to at Heart Lake when he was five weeks old. His children now camp on that same wooden floor. His family continues to reserve "their week" every year and never intend to give it up.

It is amazing how little this "camping and tramping center" has changed from 1878 to 1998. You find the same hospitality and woodsy comfort started by Henry Van Hoevenberg. Food is still

Facing page: Adirondak Loj and Nature Museum, 1997.
Photos by author.

hearty, not fancy. Lights still go out at 10 p.m. Talks prevail on Wednesday nights. Trail work continues.

This is one of the few places where the landscape and lodgings were annihilated and less than one hundred years later the forest, lake, and wildlife have been allowed to recover—actually helped to recover. The glorious lodgings have been replaced by smaller lodgings. The High Peaks Information Center greets, encourages, and educates more hikers than Henry Van Hoevenberg could possibly imagine. His prophecy came true and ADK, with its over 20,000 members, has been a fine steward of his legacies.

One sad note is that the names of the people who have protected this property are fading away. Van Hoevenberg has a plaque but his name is hardly used any more; everyone talks about the HPIC or the Marcy Dam Trail. The original Van Hoevenberg trail has been renamed the Old Marcy Dam Trail. Hicks had a lean-to but now it is simply Lean-to #5 and the Hicks Nature Trail was used only for a few years in the 1960s. The Kelsey Nature Trail was closed in 1997. The Deweys were never recognized for their stewardship of this property.

The names and faces are fading but let us remember the sacrifices and the kindness and the vision of those who have preserved this fine square mile.

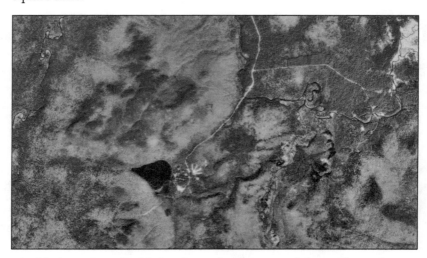

Aerial view, May 1995. Notice the marked recovery of the coniferous forest.
USGS

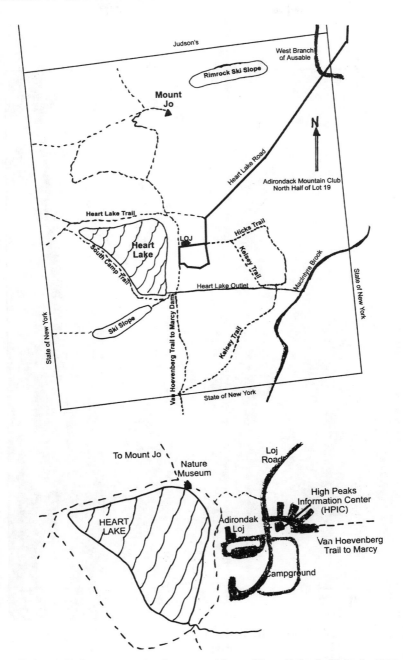

Top: Heart Lake property in the 1960s. Above: Heart Lake facilities in 1998.

Mount Jo from Mount Van Hoevenberg.
Photo by author.

Mount Van Hoevenberg

Brittle blue that mile-long
paleolithic serpent
half-way bulged at SHADY
digesting sleds and sliders

Margaret Roy,
World Cup Mt. Van Hoevenberg February 1987

IN 1904, the teenager Godfrey Dewey and veteran woodsman Henry Van Hoevenberg had great fun frolicking together in the snow and ice at the Lake Placid Club. These two friends and eight other participants did not realize that they had just made Lake Placid the first winter sports resort in America.

It was later observed, "For too long in the United States winter meant a cessation of outdoor activity and the undoing of most of the benefits gained from an outdoor life in the summer. Today, largely because of the efforts of Lake Placid, winter in the snow belt of this country is permitted to play its beneficent part in building stronger minds in stronger bodies for all who embrace what it so lavishly offers."[1]

By 1927 Lake Placid had created such a reputation that Godfrey Dewey was asked unofficially if the town would consider hosting the 1932 Olympic Winter Games. It was the intent of the Olympic Committee to hold the winter and summer games in the same country. Since Los Angeles had been awarded the summer games, the committee was looking for a U. S. resort to host the winter games.

Entrance to Mount Van Hoevenberg Olympic Sports Complex and Mount Van Hoevenberg, earlier known as South or South Meadow Mountain.

Photos by author.

Could the little village of Lake Placid (population 4,000) host such a huge international event?

The first Winter Olympics had been held in Chamonix, France, in 1924 and the second was about to be held in St. Moritz, Switzerland. Godfrey Dewey traveled to Europe to study the winter resorts and attend the 1928 games. He officially went to the Olympics as leader of the U. S. ski team but spent a lot of time studying the organization and operation of the games. Somehow he even got the job of carrying the American flag at the opening ceremony. When he returned home, he was convinced that Lake Placid could host the games in a fashion that rivaled the Europeans.[2]

Unfortunately, as Lake Placid was deciding if it wanted to be host, other towns had stepped forward to vie for the 1932 games. Bids came from Yosemite Valley and Lake Tahoe, California; Bear Mountain, New York; Duluth and Minneapolis, Minnesota; and Denver, Colorado. If all U. S. resorts were eliminated, Montreal and Oslo were waiting.

It was difficult for Dewey to persuade the committee to pick the little town of Lake Placid. The Californians desperately wanted both the summer and winter games in their state and were willing to spend huge amounts of money to make it happen. The Scandinavians refused to believe any American town could provide Olympic facilities.

By working hard, pulling strings, and hedging bets, Dewey sold his bid to the Olympic Committee. "The award was made to Lake Placid because of its pre-eminent standing as a winter sports resort, its climate and terrain, its existing sports facilities, its experience in staging winter sports, and its guarantee that the additional facilities necessary for the conduct of the Games would be provided."[3] For the first time in history, the Olympic Winter Games would be held in North America.

Two facilities missing at Lake Placid were a bobsled run and a cresta run. As Dewey had hoped, cresta was soon dropped as an Olympic event. Now Lake Placid needed only a bobsled run, but it would have to be a good one—a match for the famous European runs. Since the village of Lake Placid did not have the money to build such an expensive facility, the state had promised to build it.

The building of the bobsled run "triggered one of the shortest but most significant battles in the controversy over Forever Wild,"[4] the provision in the New York State Constitution that outlawed man-made structures on publicly-owned Forest Preserve lands. In 1929, the state legislature passed a bill authorizing funds to build, equip, and maintain a bobsled run "on lands in which any necessary easement may be provided without cost to the state,"[5] most likely privately-owned land. A few weeks later, the legislature passed a second bill, providing for the run to be built on state land.

It had been determined that the best site for the run was on state land on the western slope of the Sentinel Range due east of Lake

Above:
Presentation of the Martineau challenge cup to the USA I Four-Man Bobsled Team after their win at the 1932 Winter Olympics. Winners Billy Fiske (accepting trophy), Eddie Eagan, Clifford Gray (kneeling), and Jay O'Brien. Godfrey Dewey in fur coat, second from left.
Collection of The 1932 & 1980 Lake Placid Winter Olympic Museum.

Facing page:
Top left: USA 2 Four-Man Bobsled Team of Henry Homburger (driver), Percy Bryant, F. Paul Stevens, and Edmund Horton (brakeman). Finished second at 1932 Olympics at Mount Van Hoevenberg.
Collection of The 1932 & 1980 Lake Placid Winter Olympic Museum.

Top right: Aerial view, 1947. Mount Van Hoevenberg Bobsled Course. The upper half mile of track was still visible.
USGS

Bottom: Construction of Mount Van Hoevenberg Bobsled Run.
Collection of The 1932 & 1980 Lake Placid Winter Olympic Museum.

Placid. Because the state Constitution mandated that these be "forever kept as wild forest lands," state officials knew there might be trouble. They pushed the issue by starting to construct the run and waiting to see what happened. And things did happen! The Association for the Protection of the Adirondacks opposed the plan, contending that the run would require the illegal removal of at least 2,500 trees and that the speed, danger, and thrill of bobsledding were incompatible with land set aside as wilderness and watershed protection. The battle went to the courts.[6]

The Appellate Division found the "Bobsled Bill" unconstitutional. The case was then argued before the Court of Appeals and on March 18, 1930, it agreed. A bobsled run could not be built on state land. Judge Frederick C. Crane wrote an opinion that firmly upheld the Forever Wild clause. Trees could not be cut to make room for bobsled courses, tennis courts, baseball parks, or other recreational facilities.

Once state-owned sites were eliminated, attention turned to a proposed site on private land. A bobsled run was about to be built on Mount Jo, overlooking Heart Lake.

Godfrey Dewey now pulled a fast one. He announced that he found the Mount Jo site less than satisfactory and had been searching

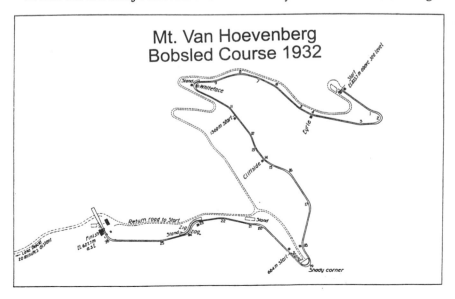

for an alternative. He proposed a new site, eight miles east of Lake Placid, known as South Mountain or South Meadow Mountain.[7] Its summit rose 2,960 feet and its north slope had the proper grade for a bobsled course. The Lake Placid Club owned the land and would give the state an easement to build the run.

The state agreed to the new site and to a change in the mountain's name to one of Olympic prominence.[8] A suggestion to call it Roosevelt Mountain was rejected. Godfrey Dewey suggested Mount Van Hoevenberg in honor of the figure who once roamed the woods and mountains surrounding the site.[9]

Mount Van Hoevenberg became the site of the first bobsled run in not only the United States but also the entire Western Hemisphere. It was used for the 1932 and 1980 Winter Olympic Games, when a luge run was added, and for many other major competitions. A Nordic ski center was also added to make the site a complete winter recreation complex.

It seems fitting that Henry's name was placed on a winter playground. For, although it was created many years after Henry Van Hoevenberg tramped through the area, he was one of the pioneers who made it happen. The III Olympic Winter Games Committee recognized this in their official report issued after the conclusion of the 1932 games:

> The Games could never have been awarded to Lake Placid if it had not been for the international standing that this resort had attained as a winter-sports center. So the history of the Games in reality goes back to that day, over a quarter of a century ago, when organized enjoyment of the sports of snow and ice and cold began where the highest peaks of the Adirondack mountains cast their shadows on the village by the two lakes.[10]

Surely, Mr. Van would be thrilled to see that the winter of 1904 set in motion a series of events that would result in Lake Placid becoming the premier winter resort of America. And, Mr. Van would like his Mount Van Hoevenberg; one side groomed for zooming bobsleds, luges and cross-country skiers, and the other side growing wild and green, watchful of South Meadow and Mount Jo.

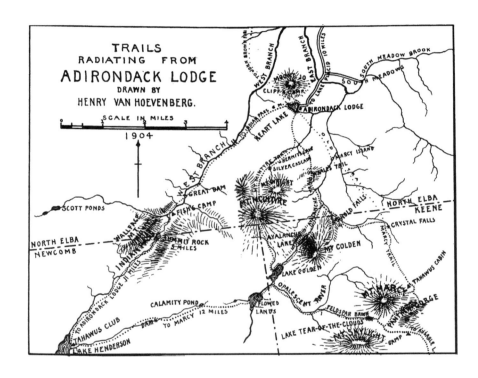

Happy Trails

Of course we weren't lost. We were merely where we shouldn't have been, without knowing where that was.

T. Morris Longstreth, *The Adirondacks*

FOR MORE THAN A HUNDRED YEARS, people have walked the trails about Heart Lake and Mount Jo and the high peaks. In 1925, Helen Bridgman wrote:

It was a cloudless day and we began work in the cool of the morning, following the trail through the woods with light steps— those deep, deep woods which greet you like a dear friend as soon as you leave the immediate vicinity of the Lodge.

Nothing is more delightful to walk over than an Adirondack trail, when the roots are not too numerous and complicated and the water course too frequently in the way. For the soil itself is in reality but powdered wood, the result of tree degeneration, held to the rock by an army of tough growths and as elastic as a hair mattress.[1]

And, in case you do not already know it, an Adirondack trail is just the place to learn about toughness and elasticity in people, too.

In those wild wood tramps you can discover character in two hours when in the city it might take two years. Human nature is down to the raw; a hint for those seeking husbands and wives. If they go

139

through a hard mountain climb with courage, patience and good manners, they are likely to go through life the same way.[2]

The hard climb to the top of Mount Marcy must have shown the true character of Henry Van Hoevenberg and Josephine Schofield and sealed their desire to spend the rest of their lives together. Henry went home from that trip hooked on Josephine and on mountain hiking. Although his romance with Josephine ended tragically, his love for mountain hiking lasted the rest of his life and changed the high peaks region forever.

It is hard to imagine the mountains without cleared trails taking us to our favorite waterfall or up our favorite peak or through our favorite mountain pass. Yet, that is the way it was. Few hiking trails existed until Henry Van Hoevenberg had the vision to see that the wider population would desire hiking if only it were made easier.

Henry Van Hoevenberg was the first to build real trails from the north into the Marcy area, where previously there were just ax blazes on trees or narrow paths that only a guide or experienced woodsman could follow. "Van Hoevenberg ordered his trails cut wide and well cleared."[3] And, he routed his trails past magnificent scenery; he did not simply build the shortest trail. He was also the first to introduce enjoyable trail food rather than the customary salt pork and hardtack.

Henry's first trail led to Marcy's summit. Next, Van Hoevenberg improved the southern portion of the existing Indian Pass trail and built a new trail at the north end that terminated at Heart Lake. In 1881, he cut a trail to the summit of the second highest mountain in the state, Mount McIntyre (Algonquin). He also built a trail up little Mount Jo.

By the end of the 1880s, Henry had opened up fifty miles of hiking trails. "From a little-visited pond in the wilderness, Heart Lake became almost overnight a major center for Adirondack mountain recreation. Van Hoevenberg must certainly be ranked as one of the major 'improvers' in this classic period of Northeastern trails history."[4]

The famous philosopher William James hiked some of those trails. In July 1898, James stayed at Adirondack Lodge to rest before heading to California for lecturing. Instead of resting, he exerted himself so much he caused irreparable damage to his heart.

Mr. Van on a mountain hike. Godfrey Dewey seated in front.
Courtesy of Mary MacKenzie.

He wrote to Mrs. James about the incident: "I have had an eventful 24 hours, and my hands are so stiff after it that my fingers can hardly hold the pen. I left, as I informed you by post-card, the Lodge at seven, and five hours of walking brought us to the top of Marcy—I carrying 18 pounds of weight in my pack."[5] He then walked down to Panther Lodge Camp and met others. He spent a sleepless but intensely memorable night there. At six in the morning, he shouldered his pack and climbed Marcy again. The group then "plunged down Marcy, and up Basin Mountain, led by C. Goldmark, who had, with Mr. White, blazed a trail the year before; then down again, away down, and up the Gothics, not counting a third down-and-up over an intermediate spur. It was the steepest sort of work, and, as one looked from the summits, seemed sheer impossible."

He wrote that he was "more fatigued than I have been after any walk." But he had not learned his lesson. The next June he returned to Adirondack Lodge. He recounted his experience in a letter to Miss Pauline Goldmark: "Once a donkey, always a donkey; at the Lodge in June, after some slow walks which seemed to do me no harm at all, I drifted one day up to the top of Marcy, and then ... found myself in the Johns Brook Valley instead of on the Lodge trail back; and converted what would have been a three-hours' downward saunter into a seven-hours' scramble, emerging in Keene Valley at 10:15 P.M."[6]

It was dark when he left the woods; he had taken no matches, coat, or food. He had fainted twice along the way but somehow kept walking. James later realized the damage he had done to his health: "This did me no good....Anyhow I was an ass, and you ought to have been there to steer me straight."

It appears that even Mr. Van's well-cleared trails required a guide or experienced woodsman or woodswoman, like Pauline Goldmark. Unfortunately, William James did not have a chance to redeem himself. The forest fires of 1903 destroyed many of the trails.

After the fires, lumbering operations moved in to clear out the burned but salvageable timber and to cut the few remaining trees that were considered fire hazards. Many of the loggers used portions of old logging roads and old hiking trails. This further hampered trail maintenance. Of course, some of the hikers used the wood roads for hiking, too.

As organizations like the Adirondack Camp and Trail Club and later the Adirondack Mountain Club worked at improving trails, building shelters, and clearing new trails, mountain hiking changed. By the 1920s, most trampers no longer hired a guide to lead them over the mountains; they carried their own supplies and simply followed the trail. Finding your way was a lot easier. For example, blue metal discs marked the Van Hoevenberg trail.

Still, hiking in the Adirondacks continued to be a wild experience. Author Roderick Peattie praised the rustic Adirondacks in 1942. He felt that the Adirondack trails and shelters were far less crowded and the countryside more nearly in its original wilderness state than in the White Mountains. He also believed the Adirondacks were wilder and more rugged than the Green Mountains. Peattie wrote: "Their appeal is especially to those who love the real wilderness, and who regard an open-front lean-to with a fireplace before it as the height of woodland comfort. Many trails thread the valleys and climb the peaks."[7]

By the end of the 1940s, most trails were maintained by the New York State Conservation Department and marked with colored discs. Signs provided clear directions at trail intersections. Peattie commented, "The chief complaint about the signs is that the distances are given in 'Adirondack miles,' which most hikers, especially the less experienced, insist are much longer than the ordinary variety."[8]

Perhaps it was those signs that brought hikers looking for the "road up Marcy." Orville Cobane set them straight.

There Ain't No Road Up Marcy!

Marcy is a majestic mountain;
I'll admit its crown is bleak!
Many people like to climb it
Because it's New York's highest peak.
I have climbed it many times
And I give this reason why:
I *walk* up that grand old mountain
Just because I cannot fly!
...*Fer there ain't no road up Marcy!*

Many times I've climbed that mountain,
Used the trails from every side,
And when asked just why I did it,
Ofttimes this I did reply:
...*Fer there ain't no road up Marcy!*

I have climbed it from Heart Lake
On my well-waxed hickory skis;
The wind on top was howling

And my nose did nearly freeze—
...*Oh, there ain't no road up Marcy!*

I have climbed it from John's Brook,
Up through mud and roots and rocks,
And when I reached the summit
Found I'd worn out both my socks—
...*Fer there ain't no road up Marcy!*

Someday you may climb Mt. Marcy,
And while you climb this grand old mound,
I would like to have you ponder
On your problems coming down—
...*Fer there ain't no road down Marcy!*

Sitting up on top this mountain,
There your pride would fairly glow:
For the view is like an eagle's
And at last you'll surely know—
Why we want no road up Marcy!

Orville N. Cobane[9]

Today, hikers arrive by the busload. The trails are worn and widened by overuse, but there still "ain't no road up Marcy!"

Although it is much smaller than Marcy, Mount Jo attracts thousands of hikers each year. The hiking tales surrounding this little peak are gargantuan.

Helen Bartlett Bridgman made a climb in 1902.

It was only Mount Jo, owned bodily by the proprietors of Adirondack Lodge, within the magic circle under their complete control, no more than a mile from base to summit, but the trail was steep. Particularly towards the last did the climber welcome conveniently placed trees and roots as a help over the boulders, though nothing mattered much in those glorious pine woods, with each step

Facing Page:
Mount Jo - March Trail. Etching by Ryland Loos.

carrying one quite obviously a little nearer the sky. I realized, then, as never before, that the heart and lungs are most drawn upon in ascent, as on the downward path it is the ankles and knees. When the top was reached I was out of breath, but not nearly so weary physically as on the swift decline.

But oh, what mattered vehement breathing when, at the apex, you caught that view! To the east, south, west, and north, mountains upon mountains, peaks and passes everywhere. Here Whiteface, with its classic contour, as cold and calm, in its symmetry and isolation, as a professional beauty; Tahawus, only a shade higher than our neighboring McIntyre, with a spur of the latter facing grim Wallface across Indian Pass. Nearer and northward were the farms and dwellings about Lake Placid, and at one's feet the perspective emphasized the heart shape of the lake, with the comforting Adirondack Lodge on its shores. And it was all so still, so exquisitely still, no one save myself on the whole mountain, and all about the unbroken forest in its Sunday quiet and calm. Like Monte Cristo, the world was mine![10]

Bartlett climbed the mountain to set herself free; others climbed it to set records. In the 1930s, marathon climbing records were set and broken in friendly competition. On July 15, 1932, Robert Marshall set out to improve Herbert L. Malcolm's record of climbing eleven peaks in one day. Marshall ascended fourteen peaks and a total of 13,600 feet in elevation. He began at Johns Brook Lodge at 3:30 A.M. and finished on the summit of Mount Jo at 10:00 P.M. For ten minutes he stayed on the summit admiring the view and reflecting on the day's accomplishments. "Mount Jo, ascended with the aid of flashlights, made an ideal climax. Northward Lake Placid was a host of lights twinkling beyond an extensive plain. Southward and westward towered the pitch black mass of Marcy, Colden, MacIntyre, Wallface and Street, while right at our feet the almost full moon was reflected in the waters of Heart Lake. All around a heavy mist was rising from the streams and meadows, giving everything an appearance as unreal as the entire perfect day had been to the normal world of twentieth century mechanization."[11]

At 10:10 Marshall descended to the Adirondak Loj, where Jed Rossman gave him a warm reception and Elise Untermeyer gave him a delicious warm supper. As he ate, his head must have been swimming with the scenes of the day and with the words exchanged with

Heart Lake and Mount Jo.
Photo by author.

West Branch of the Ausable River.
Photo by author.

a man on top of Marcy. Purely by chance, Paul Schaefer happened to be on the summit getting pictures for a film. But the meeting between the two men would have more impact than any record-breaking hike or inspiring film. Many believe that their short conversation about threats to the Adirondack wilderness stirred Marshall to work to protect wilderness all over the country and to form the Wilderness Society.

The next year Malcolm bested Marshall's record. On October 7, he started climbing Giant at 12:01 a.m. and completed his planned climbs by ascending and descending Mount Jo. However, it was only 11:06 p.m., so he climbed Mount Jo again to increase his record. He finished at 11:52 p.m., setting records for total ascent of 20,067 feet in one day, for a hiking distance of over forty miles in one day, and for climbing eighteen peaks in one day.[12]

Malcolm intentionally climbed Mount Jo twice in one day. That would seem utterly ridiculous to a few people who have climbed Mount Jo by accident. One story involves a woman who set out fishing and became lost getting back from the river. She chose a favorite method of becoming lost—the seductive, but deceptive short cut. One early morning in August 1896, the woman started to fish in the east branch of the west fork of the Ausable River about a mile from Adirondack Lodge. She fished a while, working her way along the steep banks with some difficulty. When she had gone about half a mile, she found a lumber road that she believed would provide a short cut back to the road.

The lumber road climbed on and on. She tried to figure out where she was and concluded that she was near the top of Mount Jo. She thought she could go down through the woods and come out to the lake and the Adirondack Lodge. So she struck out into the mess of trees and roots and rocks and brush. Like most who become lost on Mount Jo, she was not where she thought she was; she was on the other side.

> But I plunged on deeper and deeper into the woods, sometimes up to my ankles in mud; sometimes stepping on what appeared to be a solid, though moss-covered log, and going up to my knees into a mass of decayed wood....I don't know how long I had plunged on in this way, when I came to a stream I knew nothing about. I guessed that it was the West River.

The guides tell me I was right in that guess. Of course I knew by this time that I was lost, but I didn't dare stop to think. I had thrown away my pole some time before, but had kept my little can that I used for bait. I washed this out and all through the afternoon I stopped at the little streams and brooks and drank the cool water. I don't know what I should have done without it. When I found myself at the West River I determined to try to find the John Brown trail, of which I had heard, so I again struck off into the woods in the direction I imagined it to be. I think almost the worst times in all those long hours were when, after long struggling through the forest I would come back again and again to this same river.[13]

Just as darkness came on, she heard the sound of a horn from the guides who were searching for her. The guides came crashing through the bushes and she was found. However, she retained the experience.

It was a more dreadful experience than any one who has not tried it can imagine....I simply knew that I was astray in a pathless forest, which was, it seemed to me, illimitable, and the horror and helplessness of it all will be a nightmare to me as long as I can remember it. There were only a few touches which relieved the grim desolation. I so often came upon the trail of a deer, and a dozen times ran across the places where they had been lying, and could see the marks they had made with their feet when they got up. The birds, too, seemed to have no fear of me. Two little wrens, in particular, followed me a long distance, keeping not farther than a few feet from me, lighting on a near branch when I stopped, and flying close behind me when I moved on. But they were almost the only bright spots in an experience which seems now like a black dream.[14]

Versions of this story are repeated almost every year. Hikers seek out Mount Jo for a leisurely mountain walk and it turns out to be more adventure than they were seeking. Somehow they lose the trail and go down the north side of Mount Jo. ADK tried to help in 1960 by having L. Morgan Porter hike around the Loj trails with a bucket of yellow paint. "All the property lines will be marked with yellow paint and the trails with blue paint," he said. "Occasional ADK markers will also be used on the trails. In opening up the property lines we follow a compass course and hunt for old ax blazes and remnants of yellow paint that have endured for almost 30 years. It's lots of fun."[15]

Despite the yellow and blue paint, hikers still became lost on Mount Jo. A favorite story was told by Loj caretaker Ken Foster.

> One time a woman who was staying here left to climb Mt. Jo by herself. She wasn't back that night. It turned out that she went over the other side of the mountain and into Gonyea Swamp.
>
> We called Gary Hodgson (a DEC ranger). He went right to the swamp and came back with three lost hikers. He said, "Hey, I hit the jackpot."[16]

Sometimes visitors at Adirondak Loj become lost—not on hiking trails but in the place itself. After her first trip to the Loj, Martha Benedict concluded: "It was a perfect week-end in another world, a world of beauty where Yesterday is forgotten. The timelessness of the mountains blurs the ticking of the clock, and the infiniteness of space makes man and his worldly struggles fade into insignificance. There is peace and quiet in the mountains, on the snow-clad hills, in the silent forests, and we know we will go back."[17]

Every year thousands come back to the square mile around Heart Lake. It is still a major center for Adirondack mountain recreation. Trailheads lead to Indian Pass, Avalanche Lake, Mount Marcy, and Algonquin Peak. Also, there are many trails around Adirondak Loj. Some are heavily traveled and some are rarely used, but offer spots of historical or natural interest.

This information is not intended as a trail guide. Please refer to the Adirondack Mountain Club's *Guide to Adirondack Trails: High Peaks Region* for trail maps and safety and trail information.

Mount Jo Trail

Mount Jo is a favorite hike for families. Everyone can climb it—young children, tired parents, and those with used knees. It is a well-worn, busy trail since the small ascent of 700 feet leads to a big view of the high peaks, Heart Lake, and South Meadow.

The Mount Jo trail starts in front of the Loj, follows the Indian Pass trail past the Nature Museum, and then turns right. After a short distance, the trail splits into the Short Trail and the Long Trail. The

Short Trail is three-fourths of a mile long and has some steep sections, while the Long Trail is one mile long and offers a less strenuous approach to the summit. It was laid out by Nellie Cobane and Hal Burton. When Orville Cobane cut the trail, he had only one comment: "You must've been drunk when you blazed that trail. It goes halfway to nowheres and back again."[18]

Hikers on Mount Jo, 1997.
Photo by author.

An alternate return trail is the Rock Garden/Old Nye loop. The loop starts from the Long Trail and follows the west border of the Heart Lake property, then joins the old Nye ski trail, and finally intersects the Indian Pass Trail. It passes through some splendid patches of ferns and lichens.

Heart Lake Nature Trail

This trail is about one mile long but is best enjoyed without regard to distance or time. There are fifteen interpretive signs along the trail that you will want to stop and read. The trail starts at the Loj and heads toward the Nature Museum. The museum is a wonderful introduction to the natural history of the Adirondacks and the Heart Lake area in particular. Various displays show local flora and fauna.

Leaving the museum, head west along the Indian Pass trail, continuing straight with the Indian Pass trail at the Mount Jo intersection. At the end of the lake, veer south (left) on the Indian Pass Trail and then turn east (left) onto the South Camp trail, which heads slightly away from the shoreline into the old sugar grove.

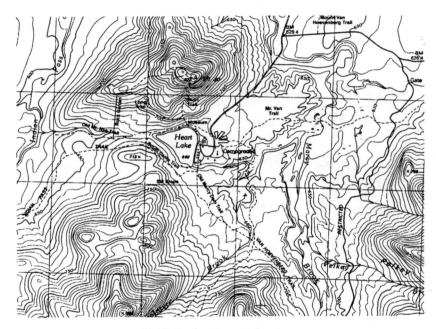

Trails in the Heart Lake Area.

Tree Trail
Over 30 species of trees can be identified on the east side of Heart Lake. A tree booklet is available at the Nature Museum.

Kelsey Nature Trail
This trail leads to a beautiful area but unfortunately is sometimes closed due to beaver "work." The trail was laid out by Dr. Orra

Phelps and is known as the Old Beaver Dams Trail. It has always been used for guided nature walks by Loj naturalists.

The trail starts behind the ranger parking area at the High Peaks Information Center. It heads into the trees just before the campground, crosses the extension of the Mr. Van ski trail, and continues east through an open pine forest. The trail comes to an area that rises to the east (left). On the hill is a beautiful section where old charred pine stumps rest on the forest floor and vibrant red pines shoot straight to the sky.

Mr. Van Trail

The Mr. Van Trail was cleared for skiing in the winter of 1967. The trail follows part of the old horse trail Henry Van Hoevenberg used every day to fetch his mail from Cascadeville. The trail is a great ski, but it is also enjoyable to walk along imagining Henry riding his horse through the trees. As you reach the meadow area there are some limited views of Mount Van Hoevenberg.

Southwest Corner Trail

An enjoyable one-mile loop can be formed by starting at the Loj and heading along the south shore on the South Camp trail. You walk through the old maple forest that escaped the fire of 1903. At the junction with the Indian Pass trail head south (left). In a short distance, a trail to the left leads to Southwest Corner Lookout. The lookout is overgrown so a view is not possible.

Returning from the lookout, head north on a trail indicating the way to the Loj. As you approach Heart Lake, the ski slope is on your left.

Another return route is the trail about one-fourth of a mile west from the lookout. This side trail heads north to the top of the Loj ski slope.

Indian Pass Trail

This trail was used by Mr. Van to escape the fire of 1903. The trail starts from the Loj, circles the north side of the lake, and then heads into an old hardwood forest. The trail passes beautiful Rocky Falls and numerous other wild spots that allow you to step back in time—to imagine the virgin forest, the great fires, the lumber camps, and the log dams.

From the Loj, it is six miles to Summit Rock at the base of Wallface Mountain.

Mount Van Hoevenberg Trail

After you climb Mount Jo a few times there is a companion peak waiting for you. It is a slightly longer hike but not as steep. This trip offers open forest, abundant bird and animal activity, rocky lookouts, and a thrilling ending, if you wish. You start hiking in a wild meadow (off the South Meadow road) and finish looking down from the top of a bobsled run.

Mr. Van trail.
Photo by author.

Fossils

*The first step in interpreting the forested Adirondack landscape is under-
standing that what we view and enjoy today is but the latest version of
several "Adirondacks" that developed and matured and then were over-
ridden by re-advancing glaciers.*

E. H. Ketchledge, *Forest and Trees*

THE ELEVATION OF MOUNT JO is 2876 feet. It does not qualify
as one of the forty-six "high peaks" or even one of the "3000"
but, it is very popular.

About 710 feet below the summit of Mount Jo lies the shoreline
of Heart Lake. Its elevation, 2165 feet, qualifies it as a high-elevation
lake. Three intermittent streams drain into the lake. It has only one
outlet, known as Heart Lake Outlet, which drains into MacIntyre
Brook and thence into the West Branch of the Ausable River.

Heart Lake is over 12,000 years old. Year after year the heart-
shaped sapphire rested quietly at the foot of Mount Jo, gathering
pollen in the spring and catching leaves in the fall. Its vast collection
of pine needles, maple leaves, and fern spores lies at the muddy
bottom.

Only within the last ten years has there been interest in those old
collections of plant parts. Scientists Donald Whitehead, Stephen
Jackson, and others studied the bottom of Heart Lake and those old
sediments revealed the history of the lake and the surrounding
forests.[1] In the core samples taken from the layers of muck they found

pollen particles and plant parts: spruce needles, a white spruce cone, paper birch fruits, white pine needles, a hemlock twig with needles, hemlock seeds, fir needles, and well-preserved beech leaves. Some of these were as much as 12,000 years old![2]

Mount Jo

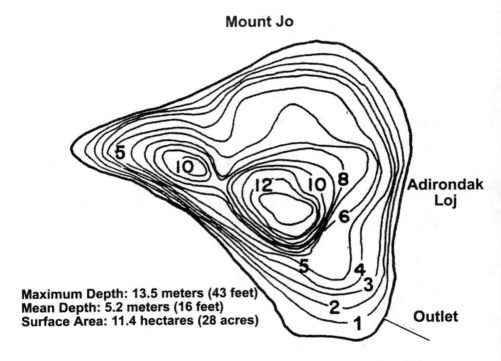

Maximum Depth: 13.5 meters (43 feet)
Mean Depth: 5.2 meters (16 feet)
Surface Area: 11.4 hectares (28 acres)

Dr. Edwin Ketchledge explains: "It so happens that any pollen or plant parts, such as leaves, twigs or fruits, that fall into these quiet waters soon sink, and in time become buried in the oxygen-depleted muck where they may remain undecayed for thousands of years. Samples from these layers then provide the evidence (hidden just 30-40 feet below us as we paddle around Heart Lake!) for constructing the sequence of when various species arrived at the site thousands of years ago."[3]

These "macrofossils" helped determine the arrival of different species at the Heart Lake watershed. Using radio-carbon technology, the scientists dated the arrival and presence of each species. This information helps us piece together the story of the "early days" at Heart Lake and Mount Jo.

Three times, glaciers advanced and swept over the forests, hills, and lakes near Heart Lake. When the area finally became free of ice about 12,500 years ago, the landscape was uncovered, the climate warmed, and plants and animals moved northward. The first immigrants to arrive were herbs, grasses, and sedges—tundra species like alpine bilberry, crowberry, and mountain alder that still survive on high summits. Soon the first tree species, white spruce, reached the slopes near Heart Lake. "White spruce was present in the vicinity of the lake...as indicated by a well-preserved cone in the lower part of the zone (~ 11,400 B. P. [Before Present])."[4] Eventually, clusters of stunted spruce spread up the mountain slopes. White spruce was present in large numbers by 10,500 years ago but declined rapidly when the climate warmed.

From 12,000 years ago until 5,000 years ago, the climate repeatedly warmed and cooled, causing species of trees to advance into the Heart Lake area from the south and then retreat. Also, there was strong competition among the plants for sunlight and patches of thin, rich soil to hold their roots.

The tamarack arrived about 11,000 years ago and established large populations. Balsam fir and paper birch followed. Between 10,000 and 9,500 years ago, the first "closed" forest appeared. Spruce, fir, tamarack, paper birch, and the newly arriving aspen spread across the slopes and formed a canopy. Paper birch dominated at this time. Except for the tamarack, these species remain in strong numbers around Heart Lake today.

About 9,000 years ago the next immigrant, the white pine, arrived. It was a very important tree for about 2,000 years, becoming even more abundant than the paper birch. Many deciduous trees appeared about this time: sugar maple, beech, oak, ash, and elm. Soon, eastern hemlock appeared and became an important conifer for many years. Populations of spruce, fir, tamarack, and especially white pine decreased. The more shade-tolerant yellow birch appeared about 6,000 years ago as the paper birch disappeared under the hemlock canopy.

By 5,000 years ago, the forest was composed of hemlock with yellow birch, sugar maple, striped maple, and beech. Then, a pathogen attacked the hemlock and caused a sharp decline of the species. Once again the balance was disturbed. With the canopy open, the birch, beech, fir, and pine increased. Conifers no longer dominated the Heart Lake countryside; for the next 2,000 years, it was prominently covered by hardwoods. Eventually, hemlock came back but it never regained its dominant position, probably because the climate had cooled.

About 2,000 years ago, the present vegetation zones were established. The climate had cooled enough to be less hospitable to white pine, hemlock, and yellow birch and more hospitable to the red spruce, which soon became the most abundant conifer.

The first evidence of settlers and farms appeared about 1860. A variety of weeds such as yarrow, ragweed, and plantain show increased populations about that time.

This is the scene that Alfred Street, Henry Van Hoevenberg, Josephine Schofield, and others gazed upon. David Burr wrote, "Many of the vallies afford a strong rich soil; and the forests are a heavy growth of oak, pine, maple, beech, walnut, butternut, birch, ash, elm, linden, cherry, fir, spruce, hemlock, and others. Much of the elevated parts are rocky and sterile."[5] According to early historian Winslow Watson, "The growth of hardwood upon this territory is in no part of the state surpassed in its size, quality, and density. Its maple, birch, cherry and beech, are as stately, and form as highly timbered woodland as in the most favored sections of the country."[6]

The forests of hardwoods and spruce, balsam, and pine had not yet experienced human disturbance. North of Heart Lake, there had been some farming and a very small amount of logging. There also had been a fire in the early 1800s. State Surveyor John Richards noted the trees "have been destroyed by the fire and wild grapes grow here" on subdivision 4 of Great Lot 10, which was very near Heart Lake.[7] There was no evidence of farming, logging, or fire in the high peaks area to the south.

Henry Van Hoevenberg changed the east shore of Heart Lake when he built the lodge and tennis courts and stables and leantos. He cut spruce and pine and hemlock trees; he cut hardwoods to burn for heating and to make furniture. He blazed trails through the pathless woods. Still, as human disturbances go, his was minimal. He cleared only the spot necessary to build the lodge and "protected hoary tree and graceful shrub alike."[8]

Around the lodge property, a few lumbering operations were active in the late 1890s. A lumber camp was just down the road at South Meadow and another was out toward Indian Pass.

View of countryside from Mount Jo.
Courtesy of Lake Placid Club Archives, Box SB-8D, Lake Placid Public Library.

Thanks to Van Hoevenberg, the Heart Lake area escaped the lumberman's ax. But he could not save it from fire. The major disturbance to the Heart Lake area came in 1903 when forest fires swept across Mount Jo. This was followed by a period of debris cleanup and logging throughout the area. Eventually, grasses, berry bushes, and shrubs grew in the open spaces. Then pioneer trees, fire cherry, quaking aspen, and birch, established themselves. Red maple and black cherry came later. Today, the original "climax" species are returning.

A combination of natural regrowth and tree plantings has generated new forests on the shores of Heart Lake and the slopes of Mount

Jo. Most of the areas surrounding the square mile were purchased by the state and became forever free from the ax.

On the northern and western sides of Heart Lake, the lower slopes are almost recovered from the fire of 1903. White pine once again stands on the shore of Heart Lake, while spruce and fir are slowly recovering on the upper slopes of Mount Jo.

The southwest part of the watershed was not greatly burned. Portions of the old sugar maple grove still stand.

The east shore of the lake has had the most intrusions and is the least returned to its "natural" state. Stands of pines were planted there in the late 1920s. Red pine occurs rarely in natural areas but has been used widely for plantations in the Adirondacks. Recently, more small trees of various species were planted to serve as samples for a "tree trail" of thirty-six species found in the Adirondack Mountains.

When you stand on top of Mount Jo, it is tempting to think you are looking at an old-growth wilderness. It is tempting to think that this is how the countryside has looked for hundreds of years—that it is standing still. In truth, this countryside illustrates change.

It shows us that "old-growth" and "virgin" forests are relative terms. When we think in terms of thousands of years, we realize that "old" is not so old. Older forests have come and gone. "Interglacial conditions have been here for only 40-tree generations of time."[9] Changes are measured in thousands of years, not decades. And, what criteria do we use to define "virgin?" The data from core samples at Heart Lake show that the makeup of the old forest changed whenever a disturbance occurred.

We also see that forests have an incredible ability to regenerate. Fire and axes and blowdown have ravaged the forest, but the slopes around Mount Jo are changing from black to green. Probably 95% of the forest you see from Mount Jo is regenerated forest, not native virgin forest. Ketchledge calls this "second-growth wilderness."

As this forest once again reaches a balance or "climax," it is tempting to think it will look this way forever. In reality it, too, is only a temporary forest stand waiting for some environmental change to shift the balance. Change may come as fire or global warming or microburst or human abuse.

Humans can cause dramatic changes in the forest. Our impact can be destructive or constructive. In ten years, our buildings and fires and lumbering and camping can destroy what it took nature 10,000 years to create. Look at the east shore of Heart Lake. For 100 years it has continually received human disturbance. In recent years, the Adirondack Mountain Club has taken efforts to minimize the impact but use appears to be reaching its limits. The continued overuse of its toilet facilities, parking facilities, and trails is causing deterioration of the Heart Lake area.

On the other hand, trees have been replanted, shelters moved back from the shoreline, old buildings removed, and traffic limited. For now, the temptation to turn Heart Lake into a mega-mall of hiking has been averted. What will it take to keep it that way?

Remember what lured Alfred Street, Josephine Schofield, Henry Van Hoevenberg, Godfrey Dewey, T. Morris Longstreth, Mrs. Van Rensselaer Cruger, Harry Hicks, and Frederick Kelsey to this place. This square mile is a rare gift. And fragile. When we come here to tramp, camp, ski, learn, and rejuvenate, we must remember to treat it kindly or we will destroy what we come here to find.

What will the view from Mount Jo look like in 10,000 years? Will this still be the very finest square mile in which to get closest to nature? When scientists dig into the mucky layers on the bottom of Heart Lake, what will they find?

What fossils will we leave in the clear pond?

Heart Lake.
Photo by author.

Notes

Clear Pond and The Bear

1 Nathaniel Sylvester, *Historical Sketches of Northern New York and the Adirondack Wilderness* (1877; reprint, Mamaroneck, New York: Harbor Hill Books, 1973), 135-6.

2 McIntyre is sometimes spelled MacIntyre. Archibald's name was McIntyre and the mountain named for him was Mount McIntyre (now Algonquin Mountain). However, MacIntyre Range and MacIntyre Brook are usually spelled with an 'a.' This book will use these spellings, except in direct quotes.

3 Mary MacKenzie, *History of the Village of Lake Placid, New York* (reprinted from *The Placid Pioneer*, Autumn 1970), 2.

4 David H. Burr, Map of the County of Essex, *Atlas of the State of New York* (1829 and 1840).

5 Arthur H. Masten, *The Story of Adirondac* (The Adirondack Museum/Syracuse University Press, 1968), 18.

6 P. Schofield to Alfred Donaldson, Nov. 29, 1918, Donaldson's Notes, Saranac Lake Library.

7 Robert F. Lucid, editor, *The Journal of Richard Henry Dana, Jr.* (Cambridge: Belknap Press of Harvard University Press, 1968), 364-373.

8 "Billy Nye: His Adventures on Land and Sea!," *The Placid Pioneer* (Summer 1970), 10. Reprinted from *Essex County Republican* (August 7, 1890).

9 Alfred Billings Street, *The Indian Pass* (New York: Hurd and Houghton, 1869; reprint, Harrison, New York: Harbor Hill Books, 1975), 139-40.

10 *A Descriptive and Historical Guide to the Valley of Lake Champlain and the Adirondacks* (R. S. Styles' Steam Printing House, 1871), 96.

11 Godfrey Dewey, "The Adirondak Loj of Long Ago," *Adirondac* (July/August 1963), 52.

12 Verplanck Colvin, *Report on the Topographical Survey of the Adirondack Wilderness of New York, For the Year 1873* (Albany, 1874), 42.

13 Ibid., 43.

14 S. R. Stoddard, *The Adirondacks: Illustrated* (Albany: Stoddard, 1874), 130.

15 Ibid.

The Early Years of Henry Van Hoevenberg

1 There are various spellings of Henry's name. The family burial monument uses the final 'h' on "Van Hoevenbergh" as Henry used through most of his life. In his later years he often dropped the 'h' from his name and his friends Godfrey Dewey and S. R. Stoddard also dropped the 'h.' The use of "burg" is an error and has a different meaning than "berg." The "Van" of a person's name is customarily written with a small 'v' on Dutch records. The American fashion is to use a capital 'V' in names. Most memorials to Henry use the "Van Hoevenberg" spelling, so this book will use that spelling, except in direct quotes.

2 Rudolf van Hoevenberg, *The van Hoevenberg Family Record* (Salt Lake City: Filmed by the Genealogical Society of Utah, 1968).

3 Ibid.; "Lieutenant Van Hoevenberg In the Revolution," *Olde Ulster; An Historical and Genealogical Magazine* 8 (1912), 76-81.

4 Register of Deaths for Catherine Gertrude Knight, Troy, New York; Arthur C. W. Kelly, *Vital Records of Niskayuna Reformed Church*, Schenectady, New York (1783-1861), 67; Federal Census for State of New York, County of Albany, City of Cohoes, 1850.

5 Federal Census for State of New York, County of Rensselaer, City of Troy, 1860.

6   *Troy City Directory* (1860-1872).
7   Thomas A. Edison, *Thomas A. Edison Papers: A Selective Microfilm Edition* (Frederick, Maryland: University Publications of America, 1985), 494, 536, and 629.
8   Frank Lewis Dyer and Thomas Commerford Martin, *Edison, His Life and Inventions* (Project Gutenberg Etext, 1997).
9   Edison, *Thomas A. Edison Papers*, 494-638.
10 Godfrey Dewey, "The Adirondak Loj of Long Ago," *Adirondac* (July/August 1963), 52.
11 Patent No. 197,504 Improvement in Parlor-Croquet Apparatus (November 27, 1877).

The Legend of 1877

1   Alfred L. Donaldson, *A History of the Adirondacks* (New York: Century, 1921; reprint, Fleischmanns, New York: Purple Mountain Press, 1992), vol. II 24-5.
2   Many writers spelled Josephine's last name "Scofield." Evidence indicates that the family name was Schofield with an 'h.' This book will use Schofield, except in direct quotes.
3   Eleanor Early, *Adirondack Tales* (Boston: Little, Brown and Company, 1939), 143-4.
4   Maitland C. De Sormo, biographical sketch in *Told Around the Campfire* (Saranac Lake, New York: Adirondack Yesteryears Inc., 1967), 3.
5   "Retrospect of Lake Placid," *Lake Placid News* (December 14, 1917), 10.
6   "One of the Many Mountain Trips," *New York Times* (Aug. 1, 1877), 3.
7   Ibid.
8   "Retrospect of Lake Placid," 10.
9   Ibid.
10 Godfrey Dewey, "Henry Van Hoevenberg, Last of Adirondack Pioneers, Answers to the Final Summons," *Lake Placid News* (March 1, 1918), 1.
11 De Sormo, biographical sketch in *Told Around the Campfire*, 3.
12 S. R. Stoddard, *The Adirondacks: Illustrated* (1903), 123-124-D.
13 William L. Wessels, *Adirondack Profiles* (Lake George, New York: Adirondack Resorts Press, Inc., 1961), 161.
14 Early, *Adirondack Tales*, 8.
15 Harry Wade Hicks, "Early Days of Adirondak Loj," *Adirondac* (Jan-Feb 1959), 5.
16 Harry Wade Hicks, "Henry Van Hoevenberg," *High Spots* (Jan 1940), 78.
17 Godfrey Dewey to Alfred Donaldson, August 8, 1918, Donaldson Collection, Saranac Lake Library.
18 Helen Bartlett Bridgman, *Conquering the World* (New York: Cloister Publishing Company, 1925), 210.
19 Ibid.
20 The following excerpts are from Julien Gordon (Mrs. Van Rensselaer Cruger), "Underbrush," *Smart Set* (September 1901), 95-99.

Miss J. J. Schofield

1   "The Last Suicide," *Niagara Falls (New York) Gazette* (October 24, 1877).
2   "The Suicide at Niagara Falls," *New York Times* (October 22, 1877), 3.
3   "The Passing of a Pioneer," *Sentinel-Review* (Woodstock, Ontario) (May 10, 1913), 1.
4   Census for Ontario, County of Oxford, Town of Woodstock, 1871; Baptist Cemetery, Woodstock, Ontario, Canada.
5   *Telegram* (Toronto) (October 17?, 1877).
6   Ibid.
7   "A Mysterious Affair," *Niagara Falls (New York) Gazette* (October 17, 1877).

8   *New York Times* (June 9, 1880), 4.
9   Op. cit.
10   "Sad End of a Woodstock Young Lady," *Woodstock Weekly Review* (Ontario) (October 19, 1877), 8.
11   "A Mysterious Affair," *Niagara Falls (New York) Gazette* (October 17, 1877).
12   Ibid.
13   Ibid.
14   "Sad Case of Suicide," *Mail* (Toronto, Ontario) (October 18, 1877), 4.
15   "Passing Away," *Woodstock Weekly Review* (Ontario) (April 12, 1878), 5.
16   Ontario Marriage Registration, Records of the Office of the Registrar General, (June 13, 1882), vol. 24, 483; *The Toronto City Directory for 1885* (Toronto, Ontario: R. L. Polk & Co., 1885), 229 and 497.

Adirondack Lodge

1   Helen Bartlett Bridgman, *Conquering the World* (New York: Cloister Publishing Company, 1925), 188.
2   Essex County Deed Record, Book 81, 467.
3   Essex County Deed Record, Book 82, 86.
4   Essex County Deed Record, Book 82, 87.
5   S. R. Stoddard, *The Adirondacks: Illustrated* (Glens Falls, New York: Stoddard, 1883), 86.
6   Bridgman, *Conquering the World*, 186-7.
7   E. R. Wallace, *Descriptive Guide to the Adirondacks* (Syracuse, New York: Watson Gill, 1882), 160(a).
8   Helen Bartlett Bridgman, "An Exploration Trip to Adirondack Lodge," *Brooklyn Standard-Union* (Oct. 13, 1901).
9   Karl Baedeker, *The United States with an Excursion into Mexico, Handbook for Travellers* (Leipsic: Karl Baedeker, 1893), 175.
10   Elizabeth Hardwick, *The Selected Letters of William James* (New York: Anchor Books, Doubleday, 1960, 1961), 148.
11   Paul Malo, "A Home to Call Our Own," *Adirondack Life* (November/December 1997), 58.
12   Wallace, *Descriptive Guide to the Adirondacks* (1882), 160(a).
13   *Elizabethtown Post* (April 17, 1879).
14   Harvey H. Kaiser, *Great Camps of the Adirondacks* (Lincoln, Massachusetts: David R. Godine, Publisher, Inc., 1982), 78 from *Encyclopedia of American Biography* (New Series, New York: American Historical Society, 1935).
15   Wallace, *Descriptive Guide to the Adirondacks* (1882), 160(a).
16   Stoddard, *The Adirondacks: Illustrated* (1883), 85.
17   Paul Malo, Professor Emeritus, Syracuse University, letter to author, October 23, 1997.
18   Bridgman, *Conquering the World*, 189.
19   Stoddard, *The Adirondacks: Illustrated* (1883), 85-6.
20   H., "A Charming New Summer Resort—Attractiveness of the Place," *Albany Sunday Press* (August, 1882); Baedeker, *Handbook for Travellers*, 175.
21   Wallace, *Descriptive Guide to the Adirondacks* (1881), Addenda.
22   Mary MacKenzie, "Castle Rustico: A Strange Chapter in Placid's History," *Lake Placid News* (May 17, 1996).
23   According to measurements made of the foundation posts.
24   Stoddard, *The Adirondacks: Illustrated* (1888), 91.
25   Stoddard, *The Adirondacks: Illustrated* (1881).

26   Stoddard, *The Adirondacks: Illustrated* (1883), 85.
27   Wallace, *Descriptive Guide to the Adirondacks* (1882), 160(2).
28   Paul Malo to author, October 23, 1997.
29   Frederic H. Comstock (probably), MS Comstock C2, 6, Keene Valley Library.
30   Wallace, *Descriptive Guide to the Adirondacks* (1880), 273.
31   Wallace, *Descriptive Guide to the Adirondacks* (1881), 160(b) and Addenda.
32   H., "A Charming New Summer Resort."
33   Wallace, *Descriptive Guide to the Adirondacks* (1882).
34   Stoddard, *The Adirondacks: Illustrated* (1888), 206.
35   Stoddard, *The Adirondacks: Illustrated* (1883), 86.
36   "How the Travelers and the Pleasure Seekers are to be Facilitated in Their Movements,"
     New York Times (Dec. 26, 1878), 3.
37   "Van Hoevenberg Died Here 20 Years Ago," *Lake Placid News* (March 4, 1938).
38   Mountain View House Guest Register, collection of Mary MacKenzie.
39   Adirondack Lodge brochure.
40   Bridgman, *Conquering the World*, 192.
41   Stoddard, *The Adirondacks: Illustrated* (1883), 86.
42   H., "A Charming New Summer Resort."
43   Stoddard, *The Adirondacks: Illustrated* (1903), 125-E.
44   Stoddard, *The Adirondacks: Illustrated* (1883).
45   Wallace, *Descriptive Guide to the Adirondacks* (1882).
46   "Van Hoevenberg Died Here 20 Years Ago," *Lake Placid News* (March 4, 1938).
47   Bridgman, *Conquering the World*, 196.
48   Archibald Campbell Knowles, *Balsam Boughs, Being Adirondack, and Other Stories* (Phila-
     delphia: Porter & Coates, 1893), 128-9.
49   "Retrospect of Lake Placid," *Lake Placid News* (December 14, 1917), 10.

The Nineteenth Century Mr. Van

1   "Retrospect of Lake Placid," *Lake Placid News* (December 14, 1917), 12.
2   Helen Bartlett Bridgman, *Conquering the World* (New York: Cloister Publishing Com-
     pany, 1925), 194.
3   Laura and Guy Waterman, *Forest and Crag* (Boston: Appalachian Mountain Club, 1989),
     216.
4   Notes from Longstreth, Donaldson Papers, Saranac Lake Library.
5   Helen Bartlett Bridgman, "An Exploration Trip to Adirondack Lodge," *Brooklyn Stand-
     ard-Union* (Oct. 13, 1901).
6   Adirondack Lodge brochure.
7   Assessment Roll of the Town of North Elba, County of Essex, 1881; Assessment Roll of
     the Town of North Elba, County of Essex, 1882.
8   Bridgman, *Conquering the World*, 200.
9   Donaldson, *A History of the Adirondacks*, vol. II 26.
10   Bridgman, *Conquering the World*, 194.
11   Memo of Tales by J. L. Harrison about Henry Van Hoevenberg, November 36, 1918.
12   "Told in Adirondacks," *Elizabethtown Post and Gazette* (Nov. 7, 1907), 3.
13   The book binder apparently made an error by adding an 'H' to the end of Henry's name.
     On the cover page that Henry likely typed himself he did not include an 'H' on Van
     Hoevenberg.
14   Patent No. 500,360 Billiard-Chalk Cup (June 27, 1893).

15   Ibid.

16   Donaldson, *A History of the Adirondacks*, vol. II 23.

17   Bridgman, *Conquering the World*, 188-9.

18   Essex County Mortgage Record, (June 26, 1885), vol. 46, 487; Essex County Mortgage Record, (October 13, 1887), vol. 47, 464; Essex County Mortgage Record, (October 25, 1893), vol. 52, 66.

19   Essex County Deed Record, Book 106, 184.

20   Essex County Deed Record, Book 110, 536.

21   Essex County Deed Record, Book 113, 18.

22   Essex County Deed Record, Book 113, 17.

23   Assessment Roll of the Town of North Elba, County of Essex, 1896; Assessment Roll of the Town of North Elba, County of Essex, 1897.

24   Stoddard, *The Adirondacks: Illustrated* (1898), 124-5-6.

25   Stoddard, *The Adirondacks: Illustrated* (1899), 126; Stoddard, *The Adirondacks: Illustrated* (1900), 126.

The Beginning of the Dewey Era

1   Wayne A. Wiegand, *Irrepressible Reformer: A Biography of Melvil Dewey* (Chicago and London: American Library Association, 1996).

2   Grosvenor Dawe, *Melvil Dewey: Seer, Inspirer, Doer* (Essex County, New York: Lake Placid Club, 1932), 20.

3   T. Morris Longstreth, *The Adirondacks* (New York: The Century Co., 1920), 240.

4   "Dr. Melvil Dewey Dead in Florida," *New York Times* (December 27, 1931), 6N.

5   *Lake Placid Club Handbook* (Morningside, New York: Lake Placid Club, 1901), 5.

6   Ibid., 7.

7   "The Adirondacks: A Winter Holiday Out of the Beaten Paths," *Boston Transcript* (February 1, 1911).

8   Godfrey Dewey, *Sixty Years of Lake Placid Club 1895-1955* (Reprint of a talk given by Godfrey Dewey, Agora Auditorium, August 4, 1955), 3.

9   Godfrey Dewey, *Sixty Years of Lake Placid Club 1895-1955*, 8.

10   Essex County Deed Record, Book 120, 438-9.

11   *Lake Placid Club Handbook* (Morningside, New York: Lake Placid Club, 1901), 94-5.

12   Ibid., 167.

13   Inventory, Adirondack Lodge, September 15, 1902, Box 51, Melvil Dewey Papers, Rare Book and Manuscript Library, Columbia University.

14   Godfrey Dewey, "Henry Van Hoevenberg, Last of Adirondack Pioneers, Answers to the Final Summons," *Lake Placid News* (March 1, 1918), 2.

15   Melvil Dewey to Henry Van Hoevenberg, January 12, 1903. Lake Placid Club Archives, Box SB-65A, Lake Placid Public Library.

The Fire of 1903

1   Harry W. Hicks, "Great Fires of 1903," *New York State Conservationist* (Aug.-Sept. 1947), 10.

2   "Adirondacks on Fire," *New York Times* (May 1, 1903), 6.

3   H. M. Suter, *Forest Fires in the Adirondacks in 1903* (Washington, D. C.: United States Department of Agriculture, Bureau of Forestry—Circular No. 26), 10.

4   William G. Distin, "Heart Lake Before the Big Fire," *Adirondac* (March-April 1964), 24-25.

5   Suter, *Forest Fires in the Adirondacks in 1903*, 11.

6   Ibid., 7.
7   Godfrey Dewey, "The Adirondak Loj of Long Ago," *Adirondac* (July/August 1963), 54.
8   Ibid.
9   Dewey, "The Adirondak Loj of Long Ago," 54.
10   *New York Times* (June 5, 1903), 2.
11   Hicks, "Great Fires of 1903," 10.
12   Alfred L. Donaldson, *A History of the Adirondacks* (New York: Century, 1921; reprint, Fleischmanns, New York: Purple Mountain Press, 1992), vol. II 27; Dewey, "The Adirondak Loj of Long Ago," 54.
13   Notes from Longstreth, Donaldson Collection, Saranac Lake Library.
14   Donaldson, *A History of the Adirondacks*, vol. II 28.
15   Dewey, "The Adirondak Loj of Long Ago," 55.
16   Op. cit.
17   Dewey, "The Adirondak Loj of Long Ago," 56.
18   Ibid.
19   Ibid.
20   Godfrey Dewey, talk made to Lake Placid-North Elba Historical Society, late 1960s. Collection of Mary MacKenzie.
21   "Flames Raging in Tinder-Dry Forests: In Adirondacks Vast Stretches of Woods Are Destroyed," *New York Times* (June 5, 1903), 1 and 2.
22   "Rain Checks Fires in the Adirondacks," *New York Times* (June 8, 1903), 3.
23   Suter, *Forest Fires in the Adirondacks in 1903*, 12.
24   "Rain Checks Fires in the Adirondacks," 3.
25   "Forest Fires Exaggerated," *New York Times* (June 16, 1903), 1.
26   "Not One Black Tract to be Seen," Comstock Scrapbook, vol. II 126, Keene Valley Library.
27   Ibid.
28   Howard Goodwin, introduction by James A. Goodwin, "Three Adirondack Summers: 1895, 1901, 1903," *Adirondac* (September-October 1971), 104-5.
29   Laura and Guy Waterman, *Forest and Crag* (Boston: Appalachian Mountain Club, 1989), 220.
30   "Rain Checks Fires in the Adirondacks," 3.
31   Melvil Dewey to J. L. Harrison, after June 3, 1903. Lake Placid Club Archives, Box SB-65A, Lake Placid Public Library.
32   Stoddard, *The Adirondacks: Illustrated* (1903), 124-D,-E.
33   Helen Bartlett Bridgman, *Conquering the World* (New York: Cloister Publishing Company, 1925), 214.

The Lake Placid Club and Mr. Van

1   Melvil Dewey to J. L. Harrison, after June 3, 1903, Lake Placid Club Archives, Box SB-65A, Lake Placid Public Library.
2   Melvil Dewey and Henry Van Hoevenberg, Memo of Agreement, July 18, 1903, Lake Placid Club Archives, Box SB-65A, Lake Placid Public Library.
3   Melvil Dewey and Henry Van Hoevenberg, Memo of Agreement, May 16, 1904, Lake Placid Club Archives, Box SB-65A, Lake Placid Public Library.
4   Mary Isabel Wright, "All's Merry at Lake Placid," *Motordom* (December 1929), 6.
5   Mary MacKenzie, "Home of the Hickories," *Adirondack Life* (Winter 1972), 8.
6   Godfrey Dewey, *Sixty Years of Lake Placid Club 1895-1955* (Reprint of a talk given by Godfrey Dewey, Agora Auditorium, August 4, 1955), 7.

7   "The Adirondacks: A Winter Holiday Out of the Beaten Paths," *Boston Transcript* (February 1, 1911).

8   Ibid.

9   T. Morris Longstreth, "Sports in the Zero Zone," *Harper's Magazine* 138 (Feb. 1919), 374.

10   Henry Van Hoevenberg to Melvil Dewey, February 22, 1905, Lake Placid Club Archives, Box SB-65A, Lake Placid Public Library.

11   *Lake Placid Club Handbook* (Morningside, New York: 1901), 22-23.

12   Fremont Rider, *Melvil Dewey* (Chicago: American Library Association, 1944), 106.

13   Alfred L. Donaldson, *A History of the Adirondacks* (New York: Century, 1921; reprint, Fleischmanns, New York: Purple Mountain Press, 1992), vol. II 287-291.

14   "Retrospect of Lake Placid," *Lake Placid News* (December 14, 1917), 11.

15   George Carroll, "Man in the Leather Suit...Henry Van Hoevenberg," *Lake Placid Club Life* (June, 1960), 7.

16   Godfrey Dewey, "Henry Van Hoevenberg, Last of Adirondack Pioneers, Answers to the Final Summons," *Lake Placid News* (March 1, 1918), 4.

17   Godfrey Dewey, talk given at Lake Placid-North Elba Historical Society, late 1960s. Collection of Mary MacKenzie.

18   Ibid.

19   Melvil Dewey to Henry Van Hoevenberg, no date, Lake Placid Club Archives, Box SB-65A, Lake Placid Public Library.

20   Godfrey Dewey, "Henry Van Hoevenberg, Last of Adirondack Pioneers," 4.

21   Henry Van Hoevenberg, letter about Adirondack Camp & Trail Club, April 25, 1911. Lake Placid-North Elba Historical Society.

22   Hicks, "Camps and Trails Near Lake Placid," *Lake Placid News* (November 11, 1921), 2.

23   Henry Van Hoevenberg, letter about Adirondack Camp & Trail Club, April 25, 1911. Lake Placid-North Elba Historical Society.

24   Godfrey Dewey, letter about Adirondack Camp & Trail Club, May 10, 1913. Lake Placid-North Elba Historical Society

25   Melvil Dewey to Henry Van Hoevenberg, October 31, 1912, Lake Placid Club Archives, Box SB-65A, Lake Placid Public Library.

26   Melvil Dewey to Henry Van Hoevenberg, October 31, 1912, Lake Placid Club Archives, Box SB-65A, Lake Placid Public Library.

27   Dewey, *Sixty Years of Lake Placid Club 1895-1955*, 5.

28   Henry Van Hoevenberg to Melvil Dewey, May 15, 1914, Lake Placid Club Archives, Box SB-65A, Lake Placid Public Library.

29   Dewey, *Sixty Years of Lake Placid Club 1895-1955*, 11.

30   Henry Van Hoevenberg to Melvil Dewey, December 10, 1914, Lake Placid Club Archives, Box SB-65A, Lake Placid Public Library.

31   Melvil Dewey to Henry Van Hoevenberg, December 14, 1914, Lake Placid Club Archives, Box SB-65A, Lake Placid Public Library.

32   Melvil Dewey to Henry Van Hoevenberg, January 19, 1915, Lake Placid Club Archives, Box SB-65A, Lake Placid Public Library.

33   Melvil Dewey to Henry Van Hoevenberg, April 13, 1917, Lake Placid Club Archives, Box SB-65A, Lake Placid Public Library.

34   "It Happened 25 Years Ago," *Lake Placid News* (June 19, 1942).

35   Kenneth Bliss, comments made during a talk by General Hugh W. Rowan at Lake Placid-North Elba Historical Society, late 1960s. Collection of Mary MacKenzie.

36   "Retrospect of Lake Placid," *Lake Placid News* (December 14, 1917), 10.

37   Dewey, "Henry Van Hoevenberg, Last of Adirondack Pioneers," 4.

38   Certificate of Death for Henry Van Hoevenberg, Town of North Elba, State of New York.

39 Dewey, "Henry Van Hoevenberg, Last of Adirondack Pioneers," 1 and 4.
40 Petition for Letters of Administration in the Matter of the Estate of Henry Van Hoeven-
    berg, Surrogate's Court, County of Essex, April 22, 1918; Affixed Affidavit of Joseph
    Knight in the Matter of the Estate of Henry Van Hoevenberg, Surrogate's Court,
    County of Essex, April 18, 1918.
41 Godfrey Dewey, "The Adirondak Loj of Long Ago," *Adirondac* (July/August 1963), 56.

The New Adirondak Loj

1   Melvil Dewey to J. L. Harrison, after June 3, 1903, Lake Placid Club Archives, Box SB-
    65A, Lake Placid Public Library.
2   Harold J. Howland, "A Winter Tramp in the North Woods," *The Outlook* 80 (June 3,
    1905), 294-5.
3   Godfrey Dewey, "The Adirondak Loj of Long Ago," *Adirondac* (July/August 1963), 56.
4   Howland, "A Winter Tramp in the North Woods," 296.
5   Helen Bartlett Bridgman, *Conquering the World* (New York: Cloister Publishing Com-
    pany, 1925), 212.
6   T. Morris Longstreth, *The Adirondacks* (New York: The Century Co., 1920), 261-4. Lynn
    was his son.
7   Ibid., 282.
8   "Placid Club Takes Over Camp and Trail Club," (June 1923?), Scrapbook 1922-32, ADK
    Headquarters, Lake George, New York.
9   Harry Wade Hicks, *How the Present Adirondak Loj was Built*, Lake Placid Club Archives,
    Box 5B-65A, Lake Placid Public Library.
10 James Goodwin to author, February 26, 1996.
11 Ed Leggett, "Adirondak Loj and the Lake Placid Club," *Adirondac* (January-February
    1963), 10.
12 Harry Wade Hicks, "Early Days of Adirondak Loj," *Adirondac* (Jan-Feb 1959), 7.
13 Hicks, *How the Present Adirondak Loj was Built.*
14 Mary B. Hotaling, "Framing a Legacy," *Adirondack Life* (April 1997), 39.
15 *Lake Placid Club Notes* (June 1927), 1687; *Lake Placid Club Notes* (November 1927), 1756;
    "Mountain-Sides Echo Shouts and Laughter of Sport Lovers in Snowy Adirondacks,"
    New York Central Lines Magazine (January 1928), 31.
16 Although the current sign on the Adirondak Loj says "Built 1928," the Loj was designed,
    built, and opened in 1927. This is confirmed by *Lake Placid Club Notes* (November
    1927 and December 1927); "Adirondak Loj of Lake Placid Club" pamphlet; "Winter
    Ascent" in *Mountain Magazine* (July 1928); "Mountain-Sides" in *New York Central
    Lines Magazine* (January 1928); "Heart Lake Before Fire" in *Adirondac* (March-April
    1964).
17 *Adirondak Loj of Lake Placid Club* (Lake Placid Club: Forest Press), 2.
18 "Winter Ascent of Mount McIntyre," *Mountain Magazine* (July, 1928), 13.
19 *Lake Placid Club News* (Jan. 17, 1930), 455.
20 *Adirondak Loj of Lake Placid Club* (Lake Placid Club: Forest Press), 5.
21 Ibid., 3.
22 "Winter Ascent of Mount McIntyre," *Mountain Magazine* (July, 1928), 13.
23 *Lake Placid Club Notes* (May 1928), 1854.
24 *Lake Placid Club Notes* (March 1929), 1960.
25 Clint Miller, "The Forgotten Man at Heart Lake," *Adirondac* (April 1981), 10.

The Adirondack Mountain Club

1   Walter Collins O'Kane, *Trails and Summits of the Adirondacks* (Boston and New York: Houghton Mifflin Company, 1928), 48-9.
2   Hal Burton, "More About Adirondak Loj," *Adirondac* (May-June 1959), 56.
3   Ibid.
4   *Adirondak Loj Club Bulletin #29* (Adirondak Loj Club Chapter of the Adirondack Mountain Club, December 1945).
5   Clint Miller, "The Forgotten Man at Heart Lake," *Adirondac* (April 1981), 11-12.
6   Edited by "Old Timer," "Come North for Sun and Powder Snow!," *Adirondak Loj Notes* (Adirondak Loj Club Chapter of the Adirondack Mountain Club, Winter 1941).
7   *Adirondak Loj Club Bulletin #28* (Adirondak Loj Club Chapter of the Adirondack Mountain Club, May 26, 1945).
8   *Adirondak Loj Club Bulletin #31* (Adirondak Loj Club Chapter of the Adirondack Mountain Club, December, 1946).
9   Schedule of Rates for Summer Season, Adirondak Loj Club, 1947.
10 *Adirondak Loj Club Bulletin #32* (Adirondak Loj Club Chapter of the Adirondack Mountain Club, May 1947).
11 Harry Wade Hicks, *How the Present Adirondak Loj was Built*, Lake Placid Club Archives, Box 5B-65A, Lake Placid Public Library.
12 *Adirondak Loj Club Bulletin #32* (Adirondak Loj Club Chapter of the Adirondack Mountain Club, May 1947).
13 Adirondak Loj Fund Committee, *A Progress Report on Adirondak Loj* (1959).
14 Ibid.
15 Bruce Wadsworth and contributors, *With Wilderness at Heart* (Lake George, New York· Adirondack Mountain Club, Inc., 1996), 82.
16 Essex County Deed Record, Book 367, 505.
17 A. Ranger Tyler, "Fund Collecting: Its Perils and Joys or How to Buy a Loj in Three Hectic Years," *Adirondac* (March-April 1962), 28.
18 Clint Miller, "Improved Adirondak Loj," *Adirondac* (March-April 1964), 22.
19 Gary Spencer, "We Really Like This Place," *Lake Placid News* (January 22, 1976), 17.
20 Ibid., 11 and 17.

Mount Van Hoevenberg

1   George M. Lattimer, *Official Report, III Olympic Winter Games, Lake Placid 1932* (Lake Placid, New York: III Olympic Winter Games Committee), 42.
2   George Christian Ortloff and Stephen C. Ortloff, *Lake Placid: The Olympic Years 1932-1980* (Lake Placid, New York: Macromedia, Inc., 1976), 49-51.
3   Lattimer, *Official Report, III Olympic Winter Games*, 48.
4   Frank Graham, Jr., *The Adirondack Park, A Political History* (Syracuse, New York: Syracuse University Press, 1984), 184.
5   Lattimer, *Official Report, III Olympic Winter Games*, 159.
6   Graham, *The Adirondack Park, A Political History*, 185-7.
7   Godfrey Dewey said the mountain was named South Mountain. Arthur Hayes said it was South Meadow Mountain. No name was found on official documents.
8   Lattimer, *Official Report, III Olympic Winter Games*, 161-2.
9   Ortloff and Ortloff, *Lake Placid: The Olympic Years 1932-1980*, 60.
10 Lattimer, *Official Report, III Olympic Winter Games*, 40.

Happy Trails

1 Helen Bartlett Bridgman, *Conquering the World* (New York: Cloister Publishing Company, 1925), 194-5.
2 Ibid., 196.
3 Laura and Guy Waterman, *Forest and Crag* (Boston: Appalachian Mountain Club, 1989), 279.
4 Ibid., 216.
5 Henry James, *The Letters of William James* (Boston: The Atlantic Monthly Press, 1920), 75.
6 Ibid., 95.
7 Roderick Peattie, *The Friendly Mountains* (New York: The Vanguard Press, 1942), 244.
8 Ibid., 245.
9 Orville N. Cobane, "There Ain't No Road Up Marcy!" *Adirondac* (July-August 1963), 50.
10 Bridgman, *Conquering the World*, 191.
11 Robert Marshall, "Fourteen in One" in *The Adirondack Reader* (Glens Falls, New York: The Adirondack Mountain Club, Inc., 1983), 415. (Reprinted from *High Spots*, October 1932.)
12 William Chapman White, *Adirondack Country* (1954; reprint, New York: Alfred A. Knopf, 1987), 13.
13 "Lost in a Great Forest," Loomis Scrapbook, vol. II 16, Keene Valley Library.
14 Ibid.
15 L. Morgan Porter, "The President Says:," *Adirondac* (July-August 1960), 67.
16 Gary Spencer, "We Really Like This Place," *Lake Placid News* (January 22, 1976), 11.
17 Martha Benedict, "My First Trip to Adirondak Loj," *Cloudsplitter* (Mar.-Apr 1945), 6.
18 Hal Burton, "More About Adirondak Loj," *Adirondac* (May-June 1959), 56.

Fossils

1 Information about the scientific studies was compiled from Stephen T. Jackson, *Postglacial Vegetational Changes Along an Elevational Gradient in the Adirondack Mountains (New York): A Study of Plant Macrofossils* (Albany, New York: New York State Museum, 1989); Donald R. Whitehead and Stephen T. Jackson, *The Regional Vegetational History of the High Peaks (Adirondack Mountains), New York* (Albany, New York: New York State Museum, 1990); Edwin H. Ketchledge, "Adirondack Insights #20. Heart Lake History," *Adirondac* (April 1989), 16.
2 Jackson, *Postglacial Vegetational Changes*, 12.
3 Ketchledge, "Heart Lake History," 16.
4 Jackson, *Postglacial Vegetational Changes*, 12.
5 David H. Burr, *Atlas of the State of New York* (New York: 1829), 22.
6 Winslow C. Watson, *The Military and Civil History of the County of Essex, New York* (Albany, New York: J. Munsell, 1869), 215.
7 Compiled by John Richards, *Field Book of Survey of the South Division of Old Military Tract No. 12, March 2, 1813*. State Archives. Evidence of a fire is also provided by the famous letter from Henderson in 1826. He wrote that his party had searched for silver south of the old Elba Ironworks "from near the River to the top of the largest burnt Cobble."
8 S. R. Stoddard, *The Adirondacks: Illustrated* (Glens Falls, New York: Stoddard, 1883), 85.
9 E. H. Ketchledge, *Forests and Trees of the Adirondack High Peaks Region* (Lake George, New York: Adirondack Mountain Club Inc., 1996), 13.

Index

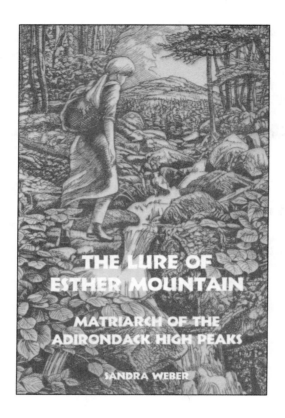

Also by Sandra Weber

Esther Mountain is the Adirondack's northernmost high peak and the only high peak named for a women. It has a unique history and unique natural features, including fir waves and a glacial cirque. Hiking directions are included. *The Lure of Esther Mountain: Matriarch of the Adirondack High Peaks* by Sandra Weber: 79 pages, illustrated, 6 x 9, quality paperback, $12.00—at bookstores or from the publisher.

Purple Mountain Press is a publishing company committed to producing the best books of regional interest as well as bringing back into print significant older works. For a free catalog of more than 300 hard-to-find books about New York State, write Purple Mountain Press, Ltd., P.O. Box E3, Fleischmanns, New York 12430-0378, or call 914-254-4062, or fax 914-254-4476, or e-mail Purple@catskill.net.